The Rocks

The 'Crystal Harmony' at Sydney Cove.

In memory of Jack Swart

INTRODUCTION

In September 1786 the English Lords of the Admiralty formulated 'a plan for effectually disposing of convicts, by the establishment of a Colony in New South Wales.' It was to be specifically a penal colony, and requests to travel out as emigrants by dispossessed American loyalists then in England following the American War of Independence wouldn't be granted. Travelling out with the First Fleet as it became known, were approximately 1400 souls. There were 212 military personnel including Governor Phillip and his staff and 28 of their wives and 17 children, and also on board were 775 convicts of whom 565 were men, 192 women and 18 children. The convicts, transported for a great variety of crimes, included Elizabeth Haywood, aged 13, transported for stealing a dress and bonnet worth seven shillings, and a chimney sweep, John Hudson, aged 12, transported for stealing some clothes.

Governor Phillip had been instructed to found his settlement at Botany Bay, but on arrival discovered that '…it did not afford a shelter from the easterly winds' and where the land around the bay wasn't 'damp and spongy' or 'a perfect swamp' there was no 'supply of fresh water, except in very small drains.' Determining to examine Port Jackson, an enclosed stretch of water a few miles north up the coast which Captain Cook had mentioned in his diary without stopping to explore, Phillip wrote that 'The different coves were examined with all possible expedition. I fixed on the one that had the best spring of water, and in which the ships can anchor… close to the shore… This cove, which I honoured with the name of Sydney, is about a quarter of a mile across at the entrance, and half a mile in length.'

The ships of the First Fleet sailed from Botany Bay to Sydney Cove, and on the evening of 26th January 1788 Phillip wrote that '…the colours were displayed on shore' and the officers 'assembled round the flagstaff (and) drank the King's health and success of the settlement…'.

On the 27th January Lieutenant King described the scene as 'A great part of the troops and convicts were landed and the latter immediately set to work clearing away the ground ready for the encampment. The place on which the settlement is to be made is at the head of a cove at the head of which a small rivulet empties itself. The shore on each side is bounded by rocks, within which there is a very fine soil, and full of trees which will require some time and labour to clear away. The Marines and Convicts are to be encamped on the west side and the Governor and Staff with his guard and a small part of the Convicts on the east side of the rivulet.'

Captain Watkin Tench of the Marines related that after the landing of the marines and convicts 'Business now sat on every brow… In one place, a party cutting down the woods; a second, setting up a blacksmith's forge; a third, dragging along a load of stones or provisions; here an officer pitching his marquee, with a detachment of troops parading on one side of him, and a cook's fire blazing up on the other.' Guards from the marine encampment on the western side of the stream were given 'directions to use force, in case of necessity, as left no room for those who were the object of the order, but to remain peaceable, or perish by the bayonet.'

The clearing of the ground was made slow, wrote Phillip, due to the 'habitual indolence of the convicts' but after ten days, when the marines and convicts had built huts and pitched tents, the women and children, who until that time had been kept on board the ships on the Cove, were permitted ashore. Arthur Smyth, surgeon on the transport *Lady Penrhyn*, described the scene, 'The men convicts got to the women very soon after they were landed and it is beyond my abilities to give a just description of the scene of debauchery and riot that ensued during the night.' The mayhem continued into the night until a sudden ferocious thunderstorm with torrential rain swept the settlement and a bolt of lightning split a tree from top to bottom in the centre of the camp killing five sheep and a pig. The following morning Phillip warned the convicts that sentries had orders to fire on any man seen in the women's camp after dark, and all men practising promiscuous intercourse would be severely dealt with.

Phillip wrote to Lord Sydney on July 9th 1788 that he was in no 'doubt but that this country will prove the most valuable acquisition Great Britain ever made…' This enthusiasm was not shared by the Reverend Richard Johnson who wrote in 1788 'In my humble opinion Government would act wisely to send out another fleet to take us all back to England or to some other place more likely to answer than this poor wretched Country, where scarcely anything is to be seen but rocks, or eaten but rats.' A sentiment agreed to by the Lieutenant Governor Major Ross, who wrote to Under Secretary Nepean on 10th July 1788, 'take my word for it, there is not a man in this place but wishes to return home… I will, in confidence, venture to assure you that this country will never answer to settle in… if ever it is able to maintain the people here it cannot be in less time than probably a hundred years hence. I therefore think it will be cheaper to feed the convicts on turtle and venison at the London Tavern than at the expense of sending them here.'

When David Collins of the First Fleet stepped ashore for the first time on the west side of Sydney Cove, it was 'from the boat literally into a wood', onto a shore lined by the rocks of 'long sandstone ledges and lintels.' It was along these natural rocky 'ledges and lintels' that the huts and tents of the marine and convict camps were built, literally on 'The Rocks', and the name of The Rocks has endured ever since for the area on the west side of Sydney Cove.

By November 1788, one of the female convicts recounted 'However, we now have two streets, if four rows of the most miserable huts you can possibly conceive of deserve that name. Windows they have none... so that lattices of twigs are made by our people to supply their places.' And four years later in 1792 an officer's wife wrote that The Rocks looked like a 'gypsy encampment, with boggy tracks wending their way around rock and precipice.'

Male convicts outnumbered the women by three or four to one during the first 50 years of settlement. On the voyage out, the First Fleet had stopped at Cape Town to take on board livestock, and the women convicts were transferred from the transport *Friendship* to other vessels to make room for the sheep, who would, Ralph Clark of the marines was convinced, make 'more agreeable shipmates than they (the women) were.' Governor Hunter found the women 'a disgrace to their sex... far worse than the men.' Michael Hayes, transported for complicity in the 1788 Irish Rebellion, who settled in Harrington Street, The Rocks with his wife Elizabeth and eight children, wrote to his sister Mary in 1802 of the local women, 'They have no shame, they talk as free as their lewd acts as an ornament to their way of living... little industry indeed is to be found amongst them, they are so accustomed to this high way of life that the most severe punishment will not restrain them.'

In the 1820s Commissioner Bigge, sent out from England to report on the administration of the colony, noted that the convicts upon being let out of their lodgings at Hyde Park Barracks, '...resort to a particular part of town called The Rocks, a place distinguished... for the practice of every debauchery and villainy... the Rocks (is) chiefly inhabited by the most profligate and depraved part of the population.'

With the establishment of sealing and whaling industries during the 1820s and 30s, Sydney became an international seaport with a reputation of being the most notorious in the world, which sailors reckoned could be smelt from a mile out to sea. Pubs such as the Hit or Miss, The World Turned Upside Down, The Hero of Waterloo, the Black Dog, the Keep Within the Compass, the Labour in Vain (which had a sign with a sailor scrubbing a Negro in a tub of water) and the Sheer Hulk did a flourishing trade in The Rocks. Alexander Harris wrote in 1847 of the Sheer Hulk, 'We found it full to suffocation of the lowest women, sailors and ruffians who supported themselves by way-laying and robbing and often murderously wounding an intoxicated sea officer... it is painful to be compelled to add, British sailors... naturally see female company where only they can find it, in the brothel.'

From the 1870s to early 1900s The Rocks were terrorised by larrikin gangs or pushes, distinctly dressed with wide-brimmed straw hats, jackets with upturned collars, pointed shoes and tight bell-bottom trousers with a white shirt billowing over a leather belt tightly strapped at the waist.

The Sydney Morning Herald wrote in 1894, 'The word larrikin is excellently descriptive of the irresponsible, mischievous, anti-social creature whose eccentric action is the result of too much mutton. This immoral will-o'-the-wisp, seized with a desire to jostle, or thump or smash, combines for the occasion with others and the shouldering shoving gang is called a push.'

A poem written in 1892, possibly by Henry Lawson, ran :

'As night was falling slowly on city town and bush
From a slum in Jones's Alley came the captain of the push
And his whistle, loud and piercing, woke the echoes of The Rocks
And a dozen ghouls came slouching round the corners of the blocks.'

On the east side of Argyle Cut were the Rocks Push, claiming to be the biggest and oldest push in Sydney and to have operated since 1841, while on the west side were the Millers Point Push, nicknamed the 'Irish Parliament' and distinguished by the white spotted red and blue bandannas they wore. In a celebrated case in June 1893, Tom Pert, a sailor from the *Royal Tar* was kicked to death outside the Gladstone Hotel on Argyle Street for giving evidence against one of the leaders. None of the attackers were convicted following the alleged intimidation of witnesses.

The residential landscape in The Rocks was described in *The Sydney Morning Herald* in 1851, '...little bunches of houses crammed together in a corner... in some places we discover people living one on the other – some literally under the earth, while perhaps the next house is built on an immense rock with the step of a doorway on a level with the adjoining chimney.' The Rocks were criss-crossed by steep alleys and lanes with names such as Frog Hollow and Black Dog Lane, where sanitary facilities were rudimentary or non-existent, causing a city official, Stanley Jevons to write in the 1850s that 'Nowhere have I seen such a retreat for filth as The Rocks.' The situation hadn't improved in the 1890s, when a social observer of the time on wandering The Rocks related 'Cold, damp, unwholesome smells assailed the nose.' Complaints of unpleasant odours or dangers to health were likely to elicit a reply from the City Council's Inspector of Nuisances that in the interests of trade no 'coercive measures' should be taken in case it would 'cripple our commerce'. 'The slums of London before the Great Fire could not have been any worse' wrote the State Member of Parliament for West Sydney, Billy Hughes, after touring the area.

At the turn of the century, wharf owners were finding up to 200 dead rats a day near the waterfront and shovelling them into the harbour. Then in January 1900, Arthur Payne, who lived at 10 Ferry Lane, complained of feeling sick on coming home from work and was diagnosed with bubonic plague. As others succumbed to the disease, in March the Government passed the 'Observatory Hill Resumption Act' and took 'supreme control' of the wharves from the head of Darling Harbour to Circular Quay including all land stretching 300 feet inland from high water mark. Under the act all privately owned land and buildings in the area, covering over 800 properties including 430 houses, 28 pubs, shops, bond stores and factories had their titles released to the 'King and Minister for Public Works' and compensation paid to the owners of just over £1,000,000. Police surrounded the district which was placed under quarantine and local residents were confined to the area and paid 6 shillings a day to assist in cleaning and disinfecting cellars, yards, factories and houses. Fences and walls were whitewashed and furniture, mattresses and piles of rubbish were heaped in the streets and burnt. Rat catchers were paid a bounty of 6d a head for every rat they caught, and told to dip the dead creature in a tub of boiling water to kill the fleas. They caught and disposed of over 45,000 rats.

Local Member of Parliament, W.J. Spruson complained that his residents were 'cooped up like fowls in a crate, exposed to every indignity and denied the opportunity to earn their living.' Work on the wharves was brought to a standstill. The disease though, continued to spread and 1200 people were confined to the Quarantine Station at North Head, having contracted the disease or come in contact with a plague victim. By the end of August when the outbreak finished, 103 had died.

A plan was drawn up by F.A.Franklin in 1900 to level completely all existing properties in The Rocks to make way for a scheme similar to Haussmann's Paris, with grand squares, avenues and wide boulevards lined with stately apartments. Franklin's scheme was considered too ambitious, and the Government didn't have the money, but a program of slum clearance took place and much of the ramshackle housing of the district was swept away and replaced by council housing. Then during construction of the Harbour Bridge in the 1920s entire streets disappeared into oblivion to make way for the southern bridge approaches.

The Rocks then remained relatively undisturbed for forty years until the 1960s when various redevelopment schemes were proposed, some of which included plans to rebuild the entire district with tall blocks of apartments and offices. The situation came to a head in the early 1970s when the Sydney Cove Redevelopment Authority started sending out notices to residents that they were to move out to allow for an 'Urban Renewal Scheme'. The residents drew up instead a 'People's Plan' arguing that The Rocks should remain as a residential and historic area separated from the adjoining Central Business District 'to revitalise the city through the return of residents' and commence a program of historic preservation of existing buildings. The residents sought help from and won the support of the Builders Labourers Federation, who for five years successfully imposed a 'Green Ban' on construction work in The Rocks to halt further demolition and development. On one particular day in 1973 four policemen were injured and 77 protestors were arrested when builders labourers occupied a site where garages were being demolished to make way for a block of flats.

The long term result of this stand is that new development has taken place in the south west section of The Rocks but much of the remainder of the district will be preserved and is gradually being restored. In sympathy with its more moderate role, 'Redevelopment' was dropped from the Authority's title and it is now known simply as the Sydney Cove Authority.

The wonderful result of this policy of preservation is that The Rocks remains as an area to be explored and enjoyed, with many houses, wharves and stores standing intact from the early decades of settlement.

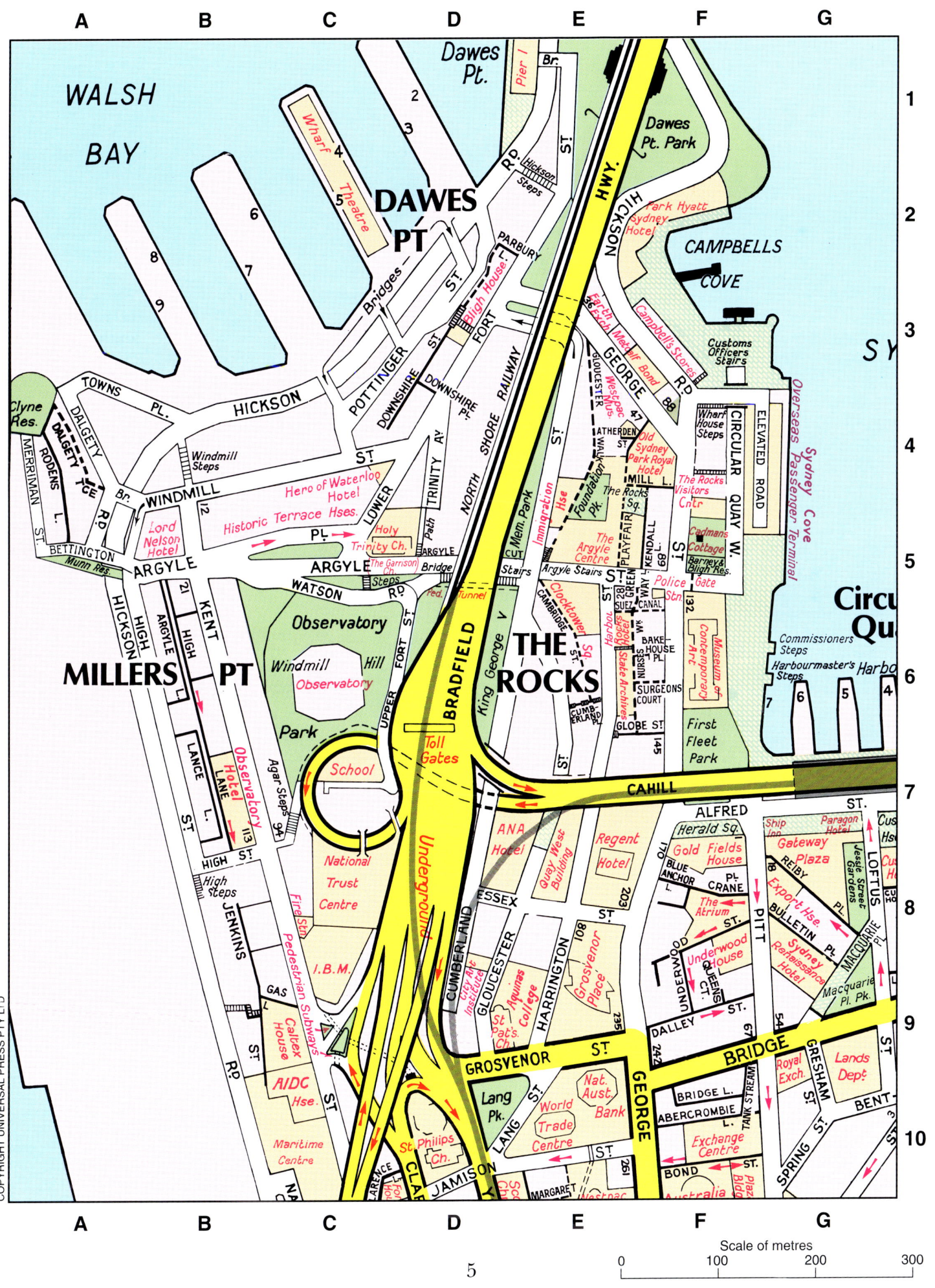

P & O's 'Island Princess' at Circular Quay (above).

Bronze birds and reptiles (above right) decorate the Tank Stream Fountain on Herald Square at the corner of George and Alfred Street.

THE ROCKS

Herald Square

This tour of The Rocks starts and finishes at First Fleet Park at the south west corner of Circular Quay. With your back to the park walk beneath the overhead railway and elevated roadway of the Cahill Expressway and cross Alfred Street to Herald Square between George and Pitt Streets. The paved square contains the Tank Stream Fountain, situated close to the original site of the mouth of the Tank Stream which ran into Sydney Cove, described by First Fleeter David Collins as '…the run of fresh water (which) stole silently through a very thick wood.' The fountain is actually a series of four fountains by sculptor Stephen Walker of convoluted shapes swarming with the life-size figures of Australian birds, reptiles and insects frozen in bronze. The seats surrounding the fountain beneath the shade of trees and bushes are filled with office workers eating their sandwiches on weekday lunchtimes. The fountain, completed in 1981, was financed by John Fairfax and Sons, publishers of *The Sydney Morning Herald* to celebrate the 150th anniversary of publication of the paper.

Turn left on George Street past the Regent Hotel then right into Essex Street. A plaque on the side of the Regent points out that this was the site of the first hanging, when a convict was strung up from a tree between the men and women's convict camps on February 27th 1788 for stealing pork and peas from settlement supplies. According to Watkin Tench 'The name of the unhappy wretch was Thomas Barret, an old and desperate offender, who died with that hardy spirit which too often is found in the worst and most abandoned class of men. During the execution the battalion of marines was under arms, and the whole of the convicts obliged to be present.' A co-offender Ralph Freeman was pardoned on condition he become the public hangman, but hesitated in his duty, and it was only after Major Ross threatened to have him shot, that he bent to his task. A thatched prison built of logs constructed on the site in 1797, burnt down in 1799 to be replaced by 'a handsome and commodious stone gaol.' This prison remained in use until 1841

Essex Street (top) was the site of Sydney's first gallows and gaol.

Harrington Street (above). The tall buildings in the background are from left to right, the Regent Hotel, Grosvenor Place, Quay West apartments and the ANA Hotel.

The Georgian style Lillyvale Cottage (top right) was built for a local schoolmaster Mr McRoberts in the 1840s.

Lang Park (above right) was the site of Sydney's first stone church, St Phillips, named after Governor Phillip, which first opened for services in 1808. The *original St Phillips was demolished and a new church named St Philip's (with one l after the Saint) was consecrated in 1856. The later church is on the right side of the picture.*

The pedestrian plaza and supporting columns of Grosvenor Place (right).

when prisoners were transferred to the new Darlinghurst Gaol.

Continue up the steeply sloping footpath of Essex Street. Note the ancient 20 metre high palm tree on the left braced with a steel harness to the side of a building to prevent it toppling over in the breeze. On the corner of Essex and Gloucester Streets, three old Victorian terraced houses have been cleverly combined inside into an old style English pub. Windows and doorframes and some of the interior fittings on the ground and first floors of Harts Pub are from the original terraced houses. Try the tasty kangaroo or chunky beef pies, served on a white china plate with a knife and fork from the good Italian cutlery service.

The ANA Hotel

At the top of Essex Street turn right along Cumberland Street past The Rocks Teppanyaki Restaurant and Lillyvale Restaurant. Lillyvale Cottage survives much as it looked in the 1840s when built for a local schoolmaster, Mr McRoberts. Built in simple colonial Georgian style with a verandah and wood shingle roof it is one of only two of its kind remaining in inner Sydney. Lillyvale Cottage and the Victorian houses that are now the Rocks Teppanyaki Restaurant and Harts Pub were all carefully restored during construction of the adjoining ANA Hotel. Walk through the stately foyer of the hotel and catch the lift to Horizons Bar on the 36th floor, a magnificent location to have a drink or coffee and enjoy the view and to get your bearings of The Rocks, Harbour Bridge, Observatory Hill and Millers Point.

Returning to the foyer of the ANA Hotel, turn left on Cumberland Street and continue walking for two hundred metres to cross Grosvenor Street to Lang Park. Grosvenor Street was named in 1889 after the Grosvenor Hotel, constructed in 1888 and demolished to make way for the Harbour Bridge approach. The street had been known as Charlotte Place, named by Macquarie after Princess Charlotte, who died in childbirth and was a daughter of George IV.

9

Lang Park

Lang Park is named after John Dunmore Lang, a Presbyterian clergyman and early advocate of an Australian republic who arrived in Sydney in 1823 intent on improving the morals of the local population after hearing from his brother George of the shocking state of behaviour then prevailing. Lang once suggested to Parliament that an address to a departing Governor include the passage 'that the moral influence that has emanated from Government House has been deleterious and baneful.' Lang lived nearby and established the Scot's Church on the corner of York and Jamieson Street. His statue is in Wynyard Park 200 metres along York Street.

A convict woman wrote in November 1788 of 'the extremity of the lines, where since our arrival the dead are buried, there is a place called the churchyard; but we hear, as soon as a sufficient quantity of bricks can be made, a church is to be built, and named St Phillip, after the Governor.' However construction of the church, which was to be built at the site of the present day Lang Park, was delayed, and two clock towers built in 1799 and 1806 were blown down in storms. When the squat church with a crenellated round tower was opened in February 1808, the locals called it 'the ugliest church in Christendom.' Attending the first service were the rebels who overthrew Governor Bligh who gave thanks to the New South Wales Corps for their support in the uprising. A peal of eight bells in the tower of St Phillips, cast at Whitechapel, London in 1794, was a gift from the Duke of Clarence, who later became George IV.

St Phillips was demolished in 1856, the same year that a new St Philips (with one 'l' after the Saint) was consecrated on the top of the hill just across York Street. Construction of the new St Philips was delayed during the 1850s when the artisans deserted enmasse to seek their fortunes on the goldfields.

Lang Park and St Philips are strictly speaking part of the City of Sydney and not The Rocks, but have been included in the tour as they are close to Sydney's oldest Catholic Church, St Patricks on Grosvenor Street, opened on St Patrick's Day 1844. Land for the church was donated by William Davis, nicknamed the 'Wexford Pikeman', transported in 1799 for complicity in the Irish uprising of 1798. Catholic priests had been banned from preaching in New South Wales until 1820, and Davis held secret masses in his house on Harrington Street on the site of which St Patrick's School building now stands. Davis died in 1843 shortly before construction of the church was completed.

Continue walking down Grosvenor Street past the ornate stucco Royal Naval House constructed in 1890. The building, recently restored, now housing the Sydney Futures Exchange, used to offer reasonably priced accommodation for servicemen and ex-servicemen.

Grosvenor Place

On the corner of Grosvenor Street and George Street stands the sturdy red-brick and sandstone Johnson's Building, with a spacious bar and restaurant called The Brooklyn on the ground floor. Read about some of the world's most famous news scoops from the assassination of President Lincoln to the relief of the siege of Mafeking in the lower Reuters Bar on George Street. The Johnson's Building caught fire during construction of the neighbouring Grosvenor Place skyscraper and was extensively damaged, but the walls of the building remained intact as a structurally sound foundation on which to rebuild the interior.

Turn left on George Street, and enter the piazza style courtyard of Grosvenor Place. The high grey office tower has been designed by Sydney architect, Harry Seidler with a generous use of public space; only a third of the area of the tower on the ground floor is occupied by supports for the building.

George Street

Continue north on George Street (towards the Harbour Bridge), pass the Regent Hotel again and go beneath the Cahill Expressway to reach a row of shops on the west side of the street. The shops are housed in a row of buildings that form one of the finest and most varied nineteenth century streetscapes in Sydney. The buildings, which nearly all contain cellars and attics, have been modified to some extent inside, but cannot be structurally altered outside except for restoration to original condition as they are listed as buildings of historical interest.

The first shops on the left are Opal Fields, D.F.S. Duty Free and The Rock Property clothing shop, occupying a site part of which was occupied for many years by the butcher W.A.Grubb, sadly no longer still in business.

On crossing Globe Street you reach The Russell Hotel on the corner, built as the Globe Hotel in 1887 on the site of a public house called The Patent Slip In. The Globe Hotel later traded as the Port Jackson, and has carried its present name since being bought by William Russell in 1900. The Russell Hotel still trades as a small private hotel. Note the French Renaissance style Widow's Walk and decorative wrought iron fence on either side of the round tower on the roof. Not too many years ago the Russell was a leniently run sailors' pub. A local gen-

George Street, (above) was the first street in Australia. The street was once called 'Spring Row' because it led to the freshwater spring at the source of the Tank Stream at present day Martin Place, then was renamed 'High Street' by Governor King and finally 'George Street' by Governor Macquarie after the "Mad Monarch" George III. The Museum of Contemporary Art is on the right.

tleman told one of the guides of *The Rocks Walking Tours* how as a young university student he had to walk home past the pub and the girls would chide him from an upstairs window and suggest that, as it was a slow time early in the evening, he was invited to come upstairs for some further education. Feeling out of his depth, he would run home.

Thirty metres along Globe Street are the State Archives, where the search room is open to the public once filling out the appropriate forms has been completed. There is often a small historical exhibition being held.

Continuing on George Street, the Fortune of War Hotel boasts holding Sydney's longest held Liquor Licence, since 1839. However the unremarkable present building was built on demolition of the original Fortune of War Inn, which traded from 1839 to 1921. A corridor on the left side of the bar leads along and up a flight of stairs to the First Fleet lounge and bistro, fronting onto the alley of Nurse's Walk.

At 135 George Street a sandstone 'Gothic Revival' building, built in ecclesiastical style looks like a bishop's residence attached to a non-existent cathedral. The building was designed in 1886 as the 'English, Scottish and Australian Bank' by architect William Wardell, who also designed St Mary's Cathedral near Hyde Park. The old bank chambers have been occupied for many years by the Ox on the Rocks restaurant.

The building at 127 George Street functioned as a Police Station from the time of its construction in 1882 until 1974. Designed by Colonial Architect James Barnet at a time when there were mob riots in The Rocks and the police were tackling the local 'push' gangs, the 'Palladian Water Gate' style of the facade was intended to personify the strength of the law. Note the lion's head holding a truncheon in its mouth in the keystone above the entrance. Was the truncheon part of the original design or was it placed there by a member of the Rocks Push following a confrontation with the law? Whatever the truth of the matter it is a fact that in the recent past the truncheon has disappeared, taken by local bucks who climbed the facade and removed it from the lion's mouth following a dare from their mates after a stag night in one of the local pubs. The old Police Station is now occupied by Australian Craftworks, 'giving the world the finest in Australian Crafts.' It is worth a wander through the old cells to look at the exquisite works in clothing, leather, wood, glass and ceramics offered for sale. Note the original cell doors and fittings, including iron rings in the cell walls from which chains hung to support a wooden slab bed which could be folded against the wall during the day.

The Museum of Contemporary Art

The Aboriginal and Tribal Art Centre shop on the 1st floor at 117-119 George Street has many aboriginal paintings, woven mats, boomerangs and other works of art for sale. Some of the finest aboriginal works of art in Australia can also be seen (but not bought) at the Museum of Contemporary Art across the road, which holds three major Aboriginal art collections.

The 'M.C.A.' as it is known was established as a result of a bequest in the will of the painter Dr John Joseph Wardell Power '...to make available to the people of Australia the latest ideas and theories in the plastic arts... by the purchase of the most recent contemporary art in the world.'

John Power, the eldest of six children and a grandson of the architect, William Wardell, was born in Sydney in

The Rocks Police Station (above) was used by the police from 1882 to 1974 and now houses the Australian Craftworks gallery.

October 1881 when the population of the town was 225,000 and of Australia 2,250,194 'excluding all full-blood Aborigines.' 'J.J.W.P.' graduated from Sydney University in 1905 with a Bachelor of Medicine and Master of Surgery, then left for London the following year to continue his studies, becoming a member of the Royal College of Physicians and working in private practice and as a research scientist on influenza vaccine at St Mary's Hospital London. Power then served in the Royal Army Medical Corps (A.M.C.) during the 1914-1918 war.

A wealthy man through the estate of his father, Power married Edith Mary James, also independently wealthy, at Paddington, London in 1915, and following the Great War was faced with a

Buildings on the west side of George Street (above). The newest building, the Fortune of War Hotel dating to the 1920's, has held a liquor licence since 1839. The pub used to trade as the Fortune of War Inn.

decision of what to do for the rest of his life. Power, who was also incidentally an accomplished pianist, decided to pursue a career as an artist. He resided in Paris where he studied at the Atelier Aroújo, then lived in Brussels, the United Kingdom and finally Jersey in the Channel Islands, travelling the world to exhibit his paintings of unusual geometrical shapes created with painstaking detail right down to the frames which he designed himself. Power died of cancer in Jersey in 1943 while the island was under German occupation, but it wasn't until 1961 on the death of his wife that the contents of his will were made public and Australia found it was to receive a fortune for the pursuit of the 'plastic arts'. The bulk of Power's enormous art collection was left for Cancer Research in England, but Edith left over 1,000 of her husband's original works of art to Australia. For a time the Power Gallery of Contemporary Art was housed as a permanent exhibition in a hall off the main quadrangle at Sydney University, then the collection moved to its present home in the former Maritime Services Board building when the Museum of Contemporary Art was established in 1989. It's interesting to reflect that it was an indirect result of stepping away from the medical profession when Power left the A.M.C. in 1918 that the M.C.A. was formed in 1987.

The M.C.A. stands on a site originally occupied by the four storey Commissariat Stores, planned by

13

Lieutenant Colonel Foveaux in 1808 when he was acting Governor of New South Wales following the overthrow of Bligh, and opened with great ceremony by Governor Macquarie in 1812. The stores, one of Sydney's oldest convict built structures, were demolished amidst unheeded public howls of protest in 1940 to make way for a headquarters for the Maritime Services Board, who control wharves, pilot boats and the administration of shipping in New South Wales. The resulting squat structure built of Maroubra sandstone, 'modified art-deco' if you like it or 'stalinist' if you don't, is considered the youngest 1930s art-deco style building in the world as it was designed in the '30s and completed without modification in the '50s. Love it or hate it, the building does though command a certain presence.

Entering the museum from the east side of George Street, there is an arty book and card shop on the ground floor. Walk through the shop and down the steps to the main entrance foyer where the simple proportions of amber and pink stonework look as clean today as when the building was completed in the early '50s. Have a glance at the high ceilinged hall adjoining the cafe on the ground floor, where the decorative theme of the interior is pink and green marble. The cafe, incidentally, serves good coffee and was voted best restaurant in the City of Sydney by American Express in 1993, who is also a sponsor of the museum. If you step out of the front doors of the museum you are confronted by the contemporary, timeless wonder of Sydney Opera House, sparkling in the sunshine, on the opposite side of Circular Quay. Now turn around to glance up at the pink granite relief above the entrance by sculptor Lyndon Dadswell, depicting labourers unloading sailing ships by sculptor Lyndon Dadswell. Directly above, near the top of the building below the clock, a propeller, ship's wheel and anchor carved in the sandstone testify to the building's original function.

Inside the museum the Members' Room occupying the former boardroom on the 2nd floor is one of the only rooms remaining in its original condition. The 1930s interior is like the inside of the *Queen Mary*, with wooden parquet floor, wooden wall panelling, glass seahorses acid-etched on the 'porthole' windows of the entrance doors and maritime motifs decorating the grills of the air-conditioning ducts.

Suffice to say that the M.S.B. building is a fitting location for the M.C.A., whose benefactor declared towards the end of his life 'It is decoration and decorative art that *really moves me most.*' You can always find something unusual, strange or distracting, including some of Power's original works, though whether you would have them on your own wall is another matter.

Crossing again to the west side of George Street, the ritzy Rockpool oyster bar occupies the ground floor of the 1860 Patrick Freehill Building at number 107. The Rocks Police Station on the corner of Argyle Street at 91 George Street occupies an Italianate style building built in 1879. The building, which pre-dates the custom built Police Station at 127 George Street by three years, originally traded as the Australasian Steam Navigation Hotel and was converted to its present use in 1983. Police serving at the counter of the new station once drank beer during their off-duty hours from a bar in almost exactly the same location in the old hotel.

The Orient Hotel on the opposite corner is built in the simple elegance of the 'Georgian' style. The hotel was originally constructed as a house and butcher's shop for James Chapman in 1844, who then licensed his premises as The Kings Arms in 1850. It has been known as The Orient since 1885. When constructed the building was right on the quay, and ships moored at the wharf across the cobbles on the other side of George Street. They included the *Cutty Sark* the fastest ever of the clipper ships, which catching the 'roaring forties' south of Cape Town would slice through the seas 'Stately as cathedrals, beautiful as terraced clouds.' Brunel's *Great Eastern*, the biggest ship in the world when it was built early in the nineteenth century and still the biggest ship afloat when it was broken up many years later, also once moored at the wharf.

Further along George Street Unwin's Stores at number 77-85 were built by solicitor Frederick Unwin in 1844 to 1846. Early tenants included Monty Tucker's American Boarding House, Theodore Matthews Nautical Instrument Maker and the Steam Packet Hotel.

At the Observer Hotel at 69 George Street note the pressed steel decoration of the ceiling in the bar. In the rear lounge of the hotel you can see a flight of sandstone steps that once led to the cellar of the Waterman's Arms Hotel built in 1844. The Waterman's Arms was demolished during the slum clearances of 1900, and the steps buried during construction of the present Observer Hotel in 1908. They came to light during conservation work in 1991. The Old Sydney Park Royal Hotel across Miller Lane was created in the interior of the former Harrington Stores.

The Rocks Visitors Centre

Cross George Street to The Rocks Visitors Centre in the old Sailors' Home building, a useful spot to pick up free leaflets about The Rocks, to learn the history of the area in one of the exhibitions or do a bit of shopping. Catch a *Rocks Walking Tour* at the centre, on which for a modest charge visitors can join a one and a quarter hour guided tour and 'See Australia's Birth Place on foot with friendly informed guides, hear factual tales of early history and Colourful Characters.'

The Sailors' Home was built by a charitable society to provide low cost accommodation for the crews of sailing ships. In the early nineteenth century under a practice known as 'crimping' sailors arriving in port were frequently met by tricksters known as 'crimps' posing as masters of registered boarding houses, who would take the sailor to a brothel or bar and get him drunk when an accomplice would rob him of his savings. The crimp would then 'sell' the indebted sailor to another ship's captain, any remaining wages the sailor received went in repaying the new captain and the sailor returned home broke. The home was built to provide the sailor with a clean, decent bed during his stay in the Port of Sydney, though if he preferred an unclean, indecent bed he could just keep walking further up the hill!

A sculpture of wharf labourers above the entrance doors of the Museum of Contemporary Art (top) is testimony to the building's original function as headquarters of the Maritime Services Board. The building at the centre of the sculpture is a rendition of the convict built 'Commissariat Stores', demolished to make way for the Maritime Services building.

The Museum of Contemporary Art (above).

A large 'Romanesque Revival' style building was designed in 1860 for the home, but due to lack of funds only the north wing was completed in 1864. Not long after the home opened in 1868, its President, Sir William Manning, intervened to save the life of Queen Victoria's son Prince Alfred, who was shot and wounded by an Irish fanatic during a picnic at Clontarf Reserve on the harbour. A donation of £500 was made by the Prince to the home as a token of gratitude.

The first and second floors of the home were originally open dormitories, which were then divided up into small cubicles arranged in two tiers around a central landing á la Alcatraz. Each cubicle, one of two of which can be seen inside, had a single narrow bed and a small cupboard for belongings.

A new separate wing for the home was built on George Street in 'Classical Revival Style' in 1926. Segregated accommodation was provided for 'natives' on ship's crews, who had their own dining, washing and sleeping facilities including 'natives' lavatories'. Providing for the worship of the sailors was the 1857 Mariner's Church next door, designed in 'classical revival' style by architect John Bibb and still standing. The church has been spoilt by an architecturally unsympathetic brick and stucco top floor added in 1909.

The Sailors' Home continued to provide accommodation for sailors until 1980.

For many years The Rocks Visitors Centre was located just along the road at 104 George Street, in the Edwardian City Morgue and Coroners Court (1904-1906), designed by Colonial Architect Walter Vernon. Before construction of the court inquests were sometimes held in the Observer Tavern across the road. One of the best known cases heard was the 'Shark Arm' case of 1935, when a missing man was identified after a shark disgorged his tattooed arm at the old Coogee Aquarium. The Morgue or 'Dead House' attached to the rear of the building was demolished when the Coroners Court moved to Glebe in 1972. Local residents were never quite sure if the high wall with broken glass on top surrounding the building was to keep people in or out.

Cadman's Cottage

Turn left outside the Sailors' Home and descend the steps immediately past it on the left to Cadman's Cottage. The cottage – the oldest dwelling in the City of Sydney – was originally built in 1816 as 'The Coxswain's Barracks' when the building was part of the Government Dockyard. The dockyard operated from 1796 to 1833 and built many vessels including the 150 ton brig *Elizabeth Henrietta* launched by Macquarie in 1816 and named after his wife. The complex was designed by convict architect Francis Greenway, who lived just across the road in George Street. Part of the original 1818 sandstone wall of the dockyard forms the retaining wall of George Street, and can be seen behind the cottage as the present-day street level runs parallel with the roof line.

George Street from the junction of Argyle Street (previous page left). The current Rocks Police Station on the corner occupies the former Australasian Steam Navigation Hotel.

The Rocks Visitors Centre (previous page right) is housed in the 1864 Sailor's Home.

Cadman's Cottage at Barney and Bligh Reserve (above), is the oldest dwelling in Sydney dating to 1816. Keys in the stonework of the Sailor's Home (visible between the trees to the right of the couple) were intended for the construction of the south bay and wing of the Sailor's Home, which was never completed due to lack of funds. If the remainder of the home had gone ahead as intended in the 1860s Cadman's Cottage would have been demolished. A statue of Governor Bligh is on the left of the picture.

The Passenger Terminal from the Sailors' Home (above left) and the Sailors' Home from the Passenger Terminal (above right). The Sailors' Home was originally constructed with a pitched slate roof, which was replaced with a flat roof when the money couldn't be found to repair the original.

The dockyard was created for the building and repairing of Government vessels and contained the offices for the administration of the Government's fleet of 20 or so boats, carrying officials, stores and convict gangs to and fro on the harbour. The boats included *The Antelope* carrying up to 58 convicts at a time between Sydney and Parramatta, *The Speedy* a fast 16 ton sloop for carrying mail and despatches on the same route and *The Shipwright's Folly* to transport logs to Sydney felled in the forests around the harbour. One of the best known sights at the time was the eight oared *Flying Fish* under the charge of 'Naval Officer' Captain John Piper (of Point Piper) which had a uniformed band playing naval airs to entertain passengers as it plied the harbour waters.

John Cadman, who had arrived in Sydney in 1798 after being transported for stealing a horse, had been an assistant to the Government Coxswain, sailing Government boats on the harbour and the cutter *Mars*, built in Newcastle and 'as fine a vessel of her size as ever built in the colony.' The *Mars* transported logs and coal to Sydney, and was shipwrecked on the coast one stormy night while in Cadman's charge. Notwithstanding this, Cadman was made Government Coxswain by Macquarie on a salary of £30 a year, received a conditional pardon, and was promoted to 'Superintendent of Government Boats', a post he held from 1827 to 1846 when he retired aged 88. In 1830 Cadman married

Elizabeth Mortimer, a 33 year old convict transported for stealing two brushes and some knives who had two daughters aged four and six. They lived together at the 'Coxswain's Barracks' and when Cadman retired the family bought the Steam Packet Inn at Parramatta where John Cadman died in 1848 aged ninety. Elizabeth Cadman later bought a paddle-wheel steamer *The Phantom*, skippered by her nephew, which was used to transport day-trippers to the salt-water baths she owned at Manly Cove.

From 1847 to 1862 Cadman's Cottage was used as a magistrate's office and cells for the Sydney Water Police, originally known as The Rowboat Guard, formed in 1789 by Governor Phillip with a force of 12 trusted convicts to patrol the harbour and prevent other convicts stowing away on departing ships. Then for over a hundred years from 1865 to 1970 the cottage was used first as a house for superintendents of the Sailors' Home – who were themselves retired captains – then as accommodation for officers from visiting merchant ships. Finally, lying vacant and derelict, the cottage was resumed and restored by the Government, and it now houses an information centre run by the New South Wales National Parks and Wildlife Service. The service offers plenty of free information including maps of walking tracks round the harbour, and the National Parks close to Sydney and throughout the state.

The 'QE 2' arriving at Sydney Cove Passenger Terminal (above). Behind the funnel of the liner is Campbells Cove, with the 'Bounty' tied up at the wharf and the Park Hyatt Hotel skirting the north west side of the Cove.

19

Governor Bligh

In the centre of the small Barney and Bligh Park next to the cottage, stands a woefully sculpted bronze statue of William Bligh (1754-1817) gazing blankly towards the Opera House. Bligh, of "Mutiny on the Bounty" fame, (also in this book under the 'Mutiny on the Bounty' heading) was later in his career appointed Governor of New South Wales. During his term of office, Bligh was overthrown by the military and clapped under house arrest for a year.

Offered the post of Governor of New South Wales in 1805, on arrival in Sydney Bligh wrote to a friend '...you can form no idea of the class of persons here who consider themselves gentlemen. The Colony seems to have been in a distracted state, and this, I am sorry to say, has been caused by the want of proper dignity at Government House.'

Bligh carried out many laudable reforms during his short term as Governor, including putting a stop to the rum monopoly, run by the local militia, the New South Wales Corps. Bligh recounted that John MacArthur (later instrumental in establishing Australia's merino wool industry) and other malcontents '...checked in the enormous practice of bartering spirits, which had principally been the almost ruin of the colony, became privately discontented; and the arch-fiend John MacArthur, so inflamed their minds as to make them dissatisfied with Government.'

Bligh later recounted in a letter, how on the 26th January 1808, (by coincidence the 20th anniversary of settlement at Sydney Cove) the mutiny took place.

'...This rebellious act was done so suddenly that in about five minutes from the time we first knew of it, Government House was surrounded with troops, Major Johnstone having brought up in battle array above three hundred men under martial law, loaded with ball to attack and seize my person and a few friends... that had been at dinner with me... they marched to the tune of the 'British Grenadiers', and to render the spectacle more terrific to the townspeople, the field artillery... was presented against the house...'.

'...I had only just time to retire upstairs to prevent giving myself up... but they soon found me in a back room (where Bligh was hiding under a bed) and, a daring set of ruffians under arms, intoxicated by spirituous liquors, which was given them for the purpose, and threatening to plunge their bayonets into me if I resisted, seized me. I was now obliged to go below, where I found the rooms filled with soldiers', where one of the leaders of the plot later boasted 'Never was a revolution so completely effected, and with so much order and regularity.'

With Bligh confined to Government House John Macarthur later wrote to his wife, 'The tyrant is now, no doubt, gnashing his teeth with vexation at his overthrow. May he often have cause to do the like.'

When Bligh left Sydney on 12th of May 1810, accompanying him on the same ship was Major Johnson, recalled to England to face court-martial for his part in the rebellion.

Governor Macquarie was sent out to restore order following Bligh's overthrow, and wrote of Bligh in a despatch to England, 'I must say that I have not been able to discover any act of his which could in any degree form an excuse for or in any way warrant, the violent and mutinous proceedings pursued against him... (but) from my own short experience, I must acknowledge that he is a most unsatisfactory man to transmit business with, from his want of candour and decision insomuch that it is impossible to place the smallest reliance on the fulfilment of any engagement he enters into...'.

The home authorities ruled that Bligh's administration had not been at fault, and he went on to enjoy a distinguished naval career, becoming an Admiral of the Blue in 1814. Johnson and Macarthur, surprisingly, were not even imprisoned for their role in the rebellion, and after being banished for a time from New South Wales both later returned to live in Sydney.

An interesting letter written by Watkin Tench, a First Fleeter whose journal is quoted elsewhere in this story, was written in September 1808 in England to Edward Macarthur, eldest son of John and Elizabeth, who had just arrived in England. '...Governor Bligh by tyranny, oppression and rapacity has drawn upon himself the just resentment of the inhabitants of the Colony and met with that spirited opposition and final defeat which I trust all unprincipled despots, whether in courts or cottages always will encounter... the decisive step that was taken was preferable to all half measures, though even the latter would from appearances have been sufficient to overawe the contemptible dastard against whom they would have been directed. The concealment under the feather bed made me smile, but did not surprise me in the least, as I had long possessed the strongest testimony from a friend who had served with Governor Bligh that he was not only a tyrant but a poltroon...'.

George Barney

The Barney of Bligh and Barney Park is Lieutenant Colonel George Barney, of the Royal Engineers who among other tasks supervised the construction of Semi-Circular-Quay in the 1840s. Construction of the quay

The 'Queen Elizabeth 2' at Sydney Cove Passenger Terminal, photographed from Dawes Point Park.

The Australasian Steam Navigation Company stores (top of picture) and Campbell's Stores (bottom of picture). The structure on the roof of the A.S.N. Co stores was built after the rest of the building was completed and houses a great water tank, installed to supply a fire control water sprinkler system installed in the 1890's.

moved the shoreline 50 metres forward from Cadman's Cottage, where the Coxswain's boats used to be pulled up onto a little sandy beach just in front of the cottage. Semi-Circular Quay was one of the last monuments to convict built labour in Sydney, as the use of convicts for public works was banned from 1845. To build the quay took seven years, involved the labour of thousands of convicts and the quarrying of tens of thousands of tons of rock from harbour headlands and islands. Barney reclaimed five hectares at the estuary of the Tank Stream, and using the *Hercules*, a locally built steam dredge and two diving bells, excavated the harbour bed to build a sea wall just inside the previous low water mark.

Sydney Cove Passenger Terminal

In front of and to the left of Cadman's Cottage is Sydney Cove Passenger Terminal, built in 1964 to receive the hundreds of thousands of migrants then arriving in Australia by ocean liner. The depth of water alongside is 10.2 metres (33 feet) and can accommodate the world's biggest passenger ships including the *QE2* and

Canberra. The site of the terminal is close to the spot where the First Fleet anchored on arrival. Phillip wrote he chose the cove as the one 'in which ships can anchor so close to the shore that at very little expense quays may be made at which the largest ship may unload.' A melancholy mural on the north wall of the arrival hall of the terminal depicting First Fleet sailors and convicts unloading supplies and raising the Union Jack was unlikely to have cheered the many migrants as they stepped ashore for the first time in Sydney. The terminal was re-modelled and shortened by architects Lawrence Neild and Partners in 1987. The work included the removal of the concrete southern vehicle approach ramp to the terminal, which had obscured Cadman's Cottage view of the water. Whether the steel framework painted in orange looking like rust inhibitor that hasn't had its top coat is an improvement is another matter. Escalators lead up to a viewing platform with a good view of the Opera House and Circular Quay.

Campbell's Stores and the A.S.N. Co building from Hickson Road. The entrance to the Earth Exchange is on Hickson Road at the lower right of the picture.

The A.S.N. Co. Building

On the landward side of the Passenger Terminal is the Australasian Steam Navigation Company building, (1883) designed by William Wilkinson Wardell (Willy Willy Wardell) in 'Flemish gabled' style. The building used to front onto Circular Quay, but the noble facade of the building was obscured by the glass and steel expanse of the Passenger Terminal. To add insult to injury the north facing facade of the building with its elegant clock-tower was partly obscured by the concrete car ramp leading to the terminal.

The A.S.N. Co. building was later used for Government Ordnance Stores and underwent a major refit in 1950 to partition the interior for Government offices and scientific laboratories which occupied the building until 1989. The interior has now been restored to its original state, and the 2nd floor level off George Street is occupied by the Ken Done Gallery, where you can see some of Ken Done's works of art at prices from $12.50 for a coffee mug to over $25,000 for an original oil painting.

Descend the Customs Officers Stairs on the right side of Hickson Road next to the road ramp to the Passenger Terminal. On the right side of the stairs is a sculpture by Lyndon Dadswell, in memory of the men of the Australian 6th Division who fought in World War II. The sculpture was unveiled by the Governor of New South Wales Air Marshal Sir James Rowland in 1983.

Campbell's Cove

As you descend the stairs to Campbell's Cove you will notice on your left a row of old storehouses, now occupied by several classy restaurants. Campbell's Stores are named after Robert Campbell, the youngest son of the Laird of Ashfield, born in Argyle, Scotland in 1769. Campbell was a partner in the firm of Campbell, Clark & Co. of Calcutta, whose first cargo sent to Sydney in *The Sydney Cove* was lost when the ship was wrecked in Bass Strait with only three survivors. Campbell then sailed out to Sydney in 1798 with a second ship called *The Hunter*, carrying a cargo of sandalwood and rum, which he was forced to sell at a reduced price to the New South Wales Corps or Rum Corps who at that time held a monopoly on the import and distribution of rum into the colony. In 1800 Campbell bought a waterfront site in The Rocks on the north east side of Sydney Cove, where he built the first commercial wharf and warehouses in Australia, importing tea, sugar and cloth into Australia, and exporting the first consignments of whale oil and seal skins. Expanding into cattle, sheep husbandry and shipbuilding, Campbell bought a property in present-day Canberra where he built his country home Duntroon, named after Duntroon Castle in Argylshire owned by a branch of the Campbell Clan. Robert lived there with his wife Sophia Palmer, daughter of First Fleeter John Palmer, Commissary General in charge of all Government Stores. Robert Campbell passed away in 1840 and is buried in the graveyard of St John's Canberra. His house is now part of the grounds of Duntroon Royal Military College Canberra.

Robert Campbell was appointed a civil magistrate and officer in charge of collections of customs duties by Governor Bligh, and sailed to London to speak for Bligh at the court martial of Major George Johnson. Later, back in Sydney, Campbell founded the first Savings Bank in Australia, known as Campbell's Bank from funds deposited with him for safe-keeping by convicts. His docks and storehouses remained in the family until sold by his grandson John Campbell for £100,000 to the Australasian Steam Navigation Co. in 1876. The A.S.N. Co. demolished Campbell's stately Wharf House dating back to 1803, to make way for the A.S.N. Co. stores. Fortunately though, the old Campbell's Stores have survived the years. The first five sandstone bays were built between 1839 and 1844, a further seven were constructed between 1854 and 1861, and an additional storey was added to the entire row about 1890. The original store houses were stone, and the extra upper level added in 1890 was built of brick, however the colour of the brick was chosen to match the colour of the sandstone and the whole structure looks in harmony. The southernmost bay was demolished to make way for a ramp for the original Overseas Passenger Terminal built in 1938. Campbell's Cove was named in honour of Robert Campbell in 1973.

The Mutiny on the Bounty

Tied to the wharf at Campbell's Cove is a full scale replica of Bligh's ship *The Bounty* built in 1979 to match the 1789 original by film producer Dino de Laurentis for the 1983 film 'Mutiny on the Bounty' starring Mel Gibson as Fletcher Christian and Anthony Hopkins as Captain Bligh. The replica was built in New Zealand at a cost of $2.5 million, and offers daily coffee, lunch and dinner cruises on the harbour.

Bligh originally joined the navy at 15 and showed such promise as a navigator and cartographer that he was invited by Cook to sail as Master of *The Resolution* on Cook's third voyage in 1776 to 1779.

Appointed to command a vessel in an expedition to the South Seas organised by Sir Joseph Banks and the Admiralty, Bligh sailed from England

The 'Bounty' on its way into Campbells Cove (above). The Opera House shells are decorated with the colours for Sydney's September 1993 bid for the 2000 Olympics.

The Waterfront Restaurant at Campbell's Stores (above).

in 1787 in a converted collier called *The Bounty* to collect breadfruit plants in Tahiti for transportation to the West Indies where they were intended to provide a cheap source of food for plantation slaves.

The expedition languished for six months in Tahiti because it was the wrong season to transfer breadfruit plants to pots, during which time some of the crew made 'some female connections' on shore. Bligh later described in a letter the people on the island :

'The women are handsome and mild in their manners and conversation, with sufficient delicacy to make them admired and beloved', which coupled with the hospitality of the men meant the sailors were tempted 'to fix themselves in the midst of plenty in the finest island in the world, where they need not labour, and where the allurements of dissipation are more than equal to anything that can be conceived.' Three weeks out from Tahiti, as Bligh later recorded in his diary '…I am now unhappily to relate one of the most atrocious acts of piracy ever committed.'

'Just before sunrise Mr Christian and the Master at Arms came into my cabin while I was fast asleep, and seizing me, tied my hands with a cord and threatened instant death if I made the least noise... Mr Christian had a cutlass and the others were armed with muskets and bayonets... I was now carried on deck in my shirt in torture with a severe bandage round my wrists behind my back.' (The original diary, with the writing smudged from drops of water after its journey in the longboat, is in the Mitchell Library in Sydney).

According to a long letter written later by Bligh to Joseph Banks, when Bligh reached the deck and the mutineers hoisted out a boat, Bligh shouted to try to rally the men and, '...I was saluted with, "Damn his eyes! blow his brains out".' But more crew supported Bligh than Christian, so to rid themselves of the majority of the loyal crew members they were forced into the boat with Bligh until it was 'so deeply lumbered that they believed we could never reach the shore, and some of them made their jokes of it.'

Christian's last words to Bligh before the boat was cast off were 'That is it, Captain Bligh, I am in hell.' The longboat sailed to the nearby island of Tofua where '...we were attacked by a multitude of Indians, in the course of which I lost a very worthy good man and the rest more or less bruised and wounded.'

Bligh determined to make for Timor, 2,500 nautical miles away, with supplies rationed to 'one ounce of bread per day and one gill of water' per person '...across a sea where the navigation is dangerous and not known, and in a small boat deep loaded with eighteen souls, without a single map, and nothing but my own recollection and general knowledge of the situation of places assisted by a table in an old book of latitude and longitude to guide me.'

Troubled by rough seas, Bligh's letter continued '...weather and sea continued very bad, and we now dreaded the nights for we were all benumbed with cold, and what added to our distress in the weak situation we were in, one of us in turns was obliged to be constantly bailing the boat in all this dreadful weather, being continually wet, and never having a dry rag about us.'

Eventually reaching the Great Barrier Reef and finding an opening through it, Bligh landed on the north coast of Australia where his crew replenished their drinking water. The men prised shellfish from the rocks and caught birds with their bare hands to make a meal cooked on a fire lit by a magnifying glass. Continuing north up the Australian coast, avoiding contact with the Aborigines who waved at them from the shore, Bligh rounded Cape York and 41 days after being cast adrift reached the Portuguese settlement on Timor with 'their limbs full of sores and their bodies nothing but skin and bones habited in rags... one half of whom could not have survived, a week longer, and some, perhaps not a few days.'

When Bligh eventually reached England he was court-martialled for the loss of his ship but honourably acquitted. A vessel called the *Pandora* was despatched to search for the mutineers, some of whom were captured on Tahiti. The *Pandora* was wrecked on the Great Barrier Reef and only 89 crew and ten mutineers survived. The senior surviving officer, Lieutenant Hayward, who had been with Bligh in the Bounty's longboat, now undertook a second epic journey of survival in a longboat to journey 1,000 nautical miles to Timor. When the mutineers returned to England, four were found

The Earth Exchange (above) is housed in a building that was constructed as an electric light power station at the turn of the century but was never used. The chimney has never emitted a puff of smoke and is now sealed.

Campbells Cove from Dawes Point Park (above).

innocent, two pardoned, one let off on a technicality and three were hanged.

After the crew of *The Bounty* had left Bligh in the longboat they sailed to Tahiti, to drop off some of the mutineers (the ones later captured) and then after picking up some Tahitian women sailed with the rest of the mutineers including Fletcher Christian to Pitcairn Island where the *Bounty* was burnt and sank. Due to an error in recording the location of Pitcairn Island on charts, it wasn't until 1808 that an American ship called there and discovered John Adams, the sole surviving mutineer. Descendants of the original Bounty mutineers live on Pitcairn Island to this day.

The modern day *Bounty* replica, though externally identical to the original *Bounty,* is a steel-hulled Lloyds class 1A ocean going vessel, with a modern navigation room with radar, sonar, a satellite navigation unit, ship to shore radio and its own fax machine. The ship has auxiliary power of two 415 horsepower turbo-charged diesel engines, a modern galley, air-conditioned dining room, reading room and sleeping quarters, and also toilets and five showers with hot and cold water. The modern *Bounty* is close to the hearts of Sydneysiders as she led the 1987 to 1988 First Fleet Re-Enactment Voyage when with nine other square rigged ships she sailed from England to Australia via the Cape of Good Hope on an eight and a half month 20,000 mile voyage for the Australian Bicentenary. Another great occasion was in 1989 when *Bounty* sailed from Sydney to Tahiti with Ron Bligh-Ware, Bligh's great, great, great, great grandson as Captain and Gerry Christian, Fletcher Christian's great, great, great, great grandson as First Officer, to re-enact the mutiny for the 200th anniversary.

The *Bounty* replica has already sailed round the world twice and covered

more miles than the original. A trip on Sydney Harbour on the *Bounty* under full sail is considered the highlight of many tourists' stay in Sydney. A replica of the seven metre (23 foot) long boat in which Bligh sailed 2,500 nautical miles with 16 other souls is tied up to the wharf next to the Bounty.

The Earth Exchange

From Campbell's Cove walk through the opening to the right of Campbell's Storehouse and cross Hickson Road to The Earth Exchange, where you can 'Journey across Australia without leaving Sydney (at) Sydney's most exciting exhibition venue.' Also, 'See Australia's largest surviving gold nugget, the Jubilee Nugget (and) the Albert Chapman Gallery, one of the world's great mineral collections.' The Earth Exchange is in the former Geological and Mining Museum, whose collection of fossils, minerals and rocks dates to the start of the Geological Survey of New South Wales in 1875. The museum is housed in a 1902 building designed by Walter Vernon for use as an electric light power station.

Technical advances at the time meant the station was too small for its projected use and additional levels were added to turn the building into a Geological and Mining Museum. The tall chimney, a well known landmark which has never emitted a puff of smoke, was in danger of being demolished some years ago, but the cost of repair was as much as the demolition cost so it remains as a folly on the landscape. Various rocks, minerals, fossils and gems are for sale in the shop on the ground floor, and one of the best views in Sydney of the Opera House can be enjoyed through the windows of the Coal Face Cafe on the 5th floor.

From The Earth Exchange return to Campbell's Cove and stroll along the board walk to the north west corner

Cannon at Dawes Point Park (above). The barrel of each cannon is decorated with the Victorian royal crest (above left). The two indentations above the crest were used as sighting marks. If the cannon were to fire today they'd blast a hole in the side of the Opera House on the opposite side of Sydney Cove.

where a few steps lead up to the swing doors of the Park Hyatt, one of Sydney's most luxurious hotels. Even if you're not rich you can pretend to be for 20 minutes as you bask in the glory of the sumptuous hotel lounge, sip a drink and admire the view of the Opera House and *The Bounty* bobbing at its mooring on Campbell's Cove.

Dawes Point

Leaving the Park Hyatt, continue on the board walk around Campbell's Cove to Dawes Point Park at the entrance to Sydney Cove opposite the Opera House. There is a great view of our national icon through the palm trees. On the waterfront next to the park on Hickson Road looking like a monument from another age is an 1880 Horse Ferry Dock.

Cross Hickson Road and walk up the grassy slope of the park. At the top, almost beneath the southern approach to the bridge are five cannon resting on wooden carriages, all that remain of the ordnance from the former Dawes Point Battery.

Lieutenant William Dawes, a trained astronomer, was recommended by the Astronomer Royal, Doctor Maskelyne, to travel out with the First Fleet to observe the transit through the southern skies of Maskelyne's Comet, due to be visible in Sydney in 1788. Dawes carried a telescope and other instruments supplied by the Board of Longitude and built a two room observatory to house them on the point on the western side of Sydney Cove. The observatory had a conical revolving roof covered with white painted canvas through which sightings were made by sliding across a shutter. Dawes called the point where he'd built his observatory Maskelyne's Point in honour of his mentor, but never did spot Maskelyne's Comet.

In Dawes' capacity as a Lieutenant in the Marines, Phillip appointed him an 'Officer of the Engineers and Artillery in the Settlement.' Dawes supervised the construction close to his observatory of eight cannon on carriages from the First Fleet flagship *The Sirius* mounted in an earthen redoubt to guard the approaches of the Cove and manned by gunners from the Sirius under Dawes' command. It was the first fortified position in Australia.

Dawes was considered by fellow First Fleeter Robert Southwell '...a most amiable man, and though young, truly religious, without any appearance of formal sanctity... He has a great share of general knowledge, studious, yet ever cheerful, and the goodness of his disposition renders him esteemed and respected by all who know him.' Dawes was a keen student of the Aborigines and compiled a vocabulary of their language. On one occasion, according to Watkin Tench, 'Mr Dawes attempted to teach Abaroo some of our notions of religion... But her levity and love of play, in a great measure defeated his efforts.' Also according to Tench, in December 1789 Dawes was sent with two others by the Governor to attempt to cross the Blue Mountains (then called the Carmarthen Mountains), 'But they found the country so rugged, and the difficulty of walking so excessive, that in three days they were able to penetrate only fifteen miles... (but when) they turned back, were further inland than any other persons before... being fifty four miles in a direct line from the sea coast.' The 'ingenious Mr Dawes' was also, according to Watkin Tench, due to the 'incompetency' of the official First Fleet Surveyor Baron Alt, 'employed on numerous occasions in surveying, measuring, and allotting... several distributions of land (and)... the plan of the town (of Sydney) was drawn, and the ground on which it is hereafter to stand, surveyed and marked out.'

Mrs Elizabeth Macarthur (wife of the 'arch fiend'), who Dawes gave piano lessons, remembered him as a man 'so much engaged with the stars that, to mortal eyes he is not always visible.' Dawes returned to England in 1791 and the following year was appointed Governor of Sierra Leone in West Africa. He later served two additional terms as Governor of Sierra Leone, then settled in the West Indies where he died at Antigua in 1837. Somehow or other the name of Maskelyne's Point never stuck, and the name of the point at the west entrance to Sydney Cove where the approach to the Harbour Bridge now stands has always been known as Dawes Point.

The battery that Dawes built was expanded and strengthened, an 1836 disposition of ordnance in Sydney showing it mounted more guns than any other defence work on the harbour, including one 2 pounder, three 6 pounders, and one 4 pounder cannon, plus two 18 pounder and fourteen 12 pounder carronades. The fort remained manned by soldiers until 1916, and was swept away entirely during the construction of the southern bridge approaches in the 1920s.

Hickson Road

At the far (west) side of Dawes Point Park, at the end of Lower Fort Street, a bridge over Hickson Road leads to Pier One on Walsh Bay, completed in 1912 twenty years before the Harbour Bridge. At the north end of the pier with beautiful views of the harbour are the *Watersedge* (on the ground floor) and *The Harbour Watch* (first floor) seafood restaurants. The tables on the outdoor verandah of *The Harbour Watch* stand on one of the original moving platforms mounted on a rail track that were used for unloading ships' cargoes.

Pier One and the neighbouring fin-

ger wharves on Walsh Bay were built at the beginning of the 20th Century by the Sydney Harbour Trust, formed in October 1900 and charged with the responsibility of rebuilding the port of Sydney to make trade more efficient. The trust had control of the hundreds of properties the government resumed following the plague, and cleared all the old wharves and buildings in a great swathe running from Dawes Point to Darling Harbour to allow the construction of new wharves. In 1907, following another smaller outbreak of plague in which 13 died, the trust was instructed to build a 'rat proof' wall inland from the docks. The result was a great rampart cut into the sandstone of Dawes Point and Millers Point, extending for three kilometres from Pier One along the length of Hickson Road to its junction with Sussex Street. The wall, rising sheer to a height of up to 60 feet (18 metres) like the bastion of a citadel, running in an unbroken line except for openings for a street, steep flights of stairs and warehouses, had a slot chiselled into it about three metres above the ground with a backward sloping edge intended to prevent rats scaling the wall.

Between the docks and the wall runs Hickson Road, built the width of a six-lane freeway in anticipation of the railway being extended from the marshalling yards at Darling Harbour to Walsh Bay. The railway was never built following the fall off in trade during the Depression, and it remains as a great highway to nowhere that

The Opera House from Dawes Point Park (above).

The southern harbour bridge piers from Lower Fort Street (left).

Dawes Point Park from beneath the southern harbour bridge approach (below). Sydney Harbour Bridge is the widest large scale bridge in the world irrespective of the method of construction. A plaque near the base of one of the left pylons pays tribute to Lieutenant Dawes, who built an observatory and battery at the point.

became a useful location for Sunday cricket matches. Hickson Road, spanned by six bridges leading to the wharves and the high ground of Millers Point, is named after the head of the Sydney Harbour Trust, Commissioner Hickson, a former Public Works Department Chief Engineer. Neighbouring Walsh Bay is named after Henry Deane Walsh, Chief Engineer of the Sydney Harbour Trust from 1901 to 1919 who supervised construction of the finger wharves. Wharves 4 and 5 have been converted into studios and The Wharf Theatre for the Sydney Dance Company and Sydney Theatre Company, while the rest, with the exception of Pier One, presently stand derelict.

The Harbour Bridge Piers

At Dawes Point Park close to the cannon of Dawes Battery stand the awesome grey granite piers of the southern Harbour Bridge pylons, decorative statements on the scale of a medieval cathedral which serve no structural purpose except to support part of the ramp for the Harbour Bridge approaches. The entire weight of the steel of the arch rests on two pairs of pins at the base of the north and south pylons. The four bearing pins, 4.2 metres long and 368 mm. in diameter, each take a thrust under full load of 20,000 tonnes. The base of the 68 x 49 metre abutment tower on which the pylons stand is hollow, and encloses an area bigger than the size of most house-blocks used as a workshop for the bridge maintenance crews. The foundation stones for the bridge, set by the Governor Sir Dudley de Chair and R.T.Ball, Secretary for Public Works on 26th March 1925, can be seen near the south east corner of the tower. From close up the grey monolithic pylons look like the enclosing wall of some high security penitentiary.

Lower Fort Street

Follow the path next to the cannon heading south beneath the Harbour Bridge approach. Marching between the tall granite support piers of the bridge approach is like marching down the aisle of some latter-day Egyptian temple, however the path leads not to some sacred altar, but to a

Bridges over Hickson Road in Millers Point (above).

ladies and gents toilet on George Street. Next door near the steps leading up to Cumberland Street is a sight guaranteed to send any Parisian misty-eyed with nostalgia, a genuine cast-iron 'pissoir', although this particular example was cast in Sydney.

Note the row of handsome three storey terraced houses on the right of Dawes Point Park at 1-19 Lower Fort Street. The elegant Georgian and Victorian houses standing on the west side of the length of Lower Fort Street and round into Argyle Place are historically and aesthetically the most significant streetscape in Australia.

Passing the Harbour View Hotel on the corner of Lower Fort Street and Cumberland Street – its view of the harbour was all but obliterated when the Harbour Bridge was built – cross the road and walk south on Lower Fort Street. One of the first houses you pass is Bligh House (1833) at number 43, built for Robert Campbell junior, second son of Robert Campbell of Campbell's Cove and, no doubt, named in memory of Governor Bligh who was a friend of the family. At 39-41 Lower Fort are a pair of town houses designed in 1835 by John Verge, architect of Elizabeth Bay House near Potts Point in the eastern suburbs. The Colonial House Museum at 53 Lower Fort Street built in 1844, maintains six rooms of the lower two floors furnished in Victorian style 'to give the impression that people of the 19th Century could well be living and working there now.' The house contains an extraordinary collection of bric a brac, including signed photographs of George VI and Queen Elizabeth (the Queen Mother) taken when they toured Australia as the Duke and Duchess of York in 1926, the personal razor set of Sir Henry Parkes, a pair of convict leg-irons and a still functioning 1878 telephone.

The Hero of Waterloo

Continue walking up Lower Fort Street to the Hero of Waterloo hotel on the corner of Windmill Street. According to James Maclehose in 1839, Windmill Street was 'the first line of communication between The Rocks and the windmills of Millers Point.'

Millers Point is named after an ex-convict John Leighton, known to the community as Jack the Miller, who owned three windmills on the high ground near the tip of Millers Point. Boats full of grain unloaded their cargoes onto a rock shelf on the harbour and the grain was winched by cable up the steep rock face. Leighton, 'a jovial though somewhat frugal man' left his home drunk one night and slipped climbing the ladder of one of his windmills, plunging to his death.

The Hero of Waterloo, whose present licensee incidentally is Ivan Nelson (no relation of the hero of Trafalgar), was built in 1843 by George Paton, a stonemason working on the nearby Garrison Church. Paton bought the land from Jonathon Clarke, owner of the Shipwrights Arms next door (built 1831, now a private house). The Hero was a favourite watering hole in days gone by for the Queen's soldiers from Dawes Battery. A tunnel now partly filled with rubble runs from the cellars of the hotel through the sandstone to the harbour a hundred metres away. The tunnel was used for rum smuggling in the old days and for press-ganging sailors, who if they had too much to drink one night were dropped through a trap door to the cellar and carried through the tunnel to wake next morning as involuntary crew aboard a wool clipper or 'cutting up blubber on a year's whaling cruise.' Hero T-shirts, playing cards and cigarette lighters are available for sale at the bar.

Victorian terraces line Lower Fort Street (above left).

The "Great Wall" of The Rocks (above) was constructed following outbreaks of the plague in 1900 and 1907 in an attempt to prevent rats penetrating inland from the docks. A zig-zag groove cut in the lower wall was intended to prevent rats scaling the heights.

Arthur Payne, the first person diagnosed with the plague in 1900, lived at Ferry Lane (above), which leads off the corner of Lower Fort Street and Windmill Street.

The 1843 'Hero of Waterloo' (above right) was a popular drinking location for the red coats of Dawes Point Battery.

The Garrison Church

Continue up Lower Fort Street to the Garrison Church on Argyle Place. Note the same 'sparrow-pecked' style of stonework that was used on the Hero of Waterloo. The Garrison Church, whose official title is the Church of Holy Trinity, was commenced by Henry Ginn in 1840 and enlarged by Edmund Blacket between 1855 and 1874. The stained glass east window, crafted by Charles Clutterbuck of Essex, England and considered one of the finest in Australia, was a gift of Dr James Mitchell (father of David Scott Mitchell of Mitchell Library fame) as a memorial to his wife's parents. A spire in the original design was never completed, though for many years courses of stonework were left protruding on either side of the entrance arch in the vain hope that one day it would. Two thousand pounds from the Tower Fund was eventually used to repair the roof of the church and church school in 1938.

Between 1840 and 1880 the church was attended by British Redcoats (50th Queen's Own Regiment) from Dawes Battery, and has held commemorative military services ever since. The interior is lined by regimental flags, and plaques on the walls dedicated to the men of various British and Australian army units can be read by following the Memorial Ambulatory around the side aisles. 'Tell them of us and say, for your tomorrow we gave our today.' The church has a special atmosphere that isn't broken as you step out of the entrance to be greeted by the peaceful scene of Argyle Green with its terraced houses and a flight of stone steps leading up to Observatory Hill. It's a scene that has remained unchanged for a hundred years or more, and the spell is only broken by the sound of the hum of traffic on the Harbour Bridge and the sight of parked cars around the green.

Sir Edmund Barton (1849-1920), the first Australian Prime Minister following Federation in 1901, attended the Parish School next to the church, which was used as a school from 1846 to 1942. The old school is now the Parish Hall, containing the very interesting Combined Services Museum, with memorabilia and uniforms on display dating from the First World War to the Gulf War.

Argyle Cut

On Argyle Street next to the Garrison Church is the Argyle Cut through the sandstone ridge of The Rocks. During the early decades of settlement the only access by road between The Rocks and Millers Point was via Dawes Point. The rocky ridge across the spine of land between the two localities divided Argyle Street into 'two divisions... separated by a precipice of considerable height.' In 1843 Governor Burke sent convicts from Hyde Park Barracks to make a cutting through the rock by hand, using picks, hammers and chisels. They were urged on by a cruel overseer who would chant to his charges as they laboured 'by the Grace of God and the strong arm of the flogger, I'll

Argyle Cut (above) was commenced by convict labour in 1843 and eventually completed by municipal labour in 1859.

Slender pillars line the aisle of the Garrison Church (above). The church was designed by Edmund Blacket, a self-taught architect who had been prevented from studying as an architect by his father who was a London merchant. Blacket was travelling out from England to emigrate to New Zealand in the 1840s then changed his mind and settled in Sydney when his ship stopped here.

give yer fifty before breakfast tomorrer.' Work on the cut lapsed with a ban on the use of convicts for Public Works in 1845, and the cut was eventually completed by Municipal Labour with the use of explosives in 1859.

Originally just a cart's width wide, then later widened, the cut used to be spanned by three bridges to link the streets on either side of the cut, two of which went to make way for the Harbour Bridge approach. Clumps of maidenhair ferns cling to the damp cracks and crevices of the sandstone of the cut.

Argyle Place

Don't go down the cut but cross Argyle Green to the Lord Nelson Hotel on the corner of Kent Street. On the way note number 50 Argyle Place dating to about 1850, and numbers 52-60 dating to the 1840s. Where the asphalt of the street has crumbled away wooden 'cobbles' are exposed; hardwood blocks soaked in tar that were used to pave Sydney's streets from the 1880s to 1920s. Just down the hill from the Lord Nelson at the corner of Windmill Street, you can look across to Moore's Stores on the harbour, origi-

The Garrison Church (above).

nally built by William Long in 1835, and named after Captain Joseph Moore who ran the stores and wharf. Much of the gold exported from Sydney in the 1850s left from the wharf. Moore's son Henry was Sydney agent for the Peninsula & Orient Line (P & O), whose first mail steamer the *S.S. Chusan* arrived at Moore's Wharf in 1852 carrying the first direct shipment of mail brought out under contract. People wept in the streets as they read letters from home sent just a few weeks ago. In 1855 the first steam locomotives for use on Australia's first railway line from Sydney to Parramatta were unloaded at Moore's Wharf and hauled up the steep hill on winches. The old wharf was moved stone by stone to its present location in the 1970s when its original site was needed for the container terminal on the north west corner of Walsh Bay.

The Lord Nelson Hotel

The white sandstone Lord Nelson Hotel carries the honour of being Sydney's oldest hotel. The first landlord was an ex-convict plasterer, William Wells, who erected the

39

Clockwise from top left: Argyle Place, steps from Argyle Street to Watson Road were cut in 1866, the verandahed house at 50 Argyle Place dates to the 1850s and terraces near the east corner of Argyle Place.

building as his home in 1834 using sandstone blocks quarried from the base of Observatory Hill. In 1838 Wells bought a pub across the road on the north east corner of Kent Street and Argyle Street called The Sailor's Return which he renamed The Quarrymen's Arms. In 1841 he sold that pub and applied for a liquor licence for his home which he then called The Lord Nelson. A pub over the road called The Napoleon ran in competition to the Lord Nelson for a time in the nineteenth century.

These days the Lord Nelson is advertised as 'The pub that restored Nelson's eyesight.' The pub brews its own beers in-house, offering a choice of Trafalgar Pale Ale, Victory Bitter, Quayle Ale or Old Admiral, 6.7% proof brewed in 'traditional dogbolter style – to be taken with great respect. Unfortunately the Nelson's Blood Stout is no longer available. Various mementoes of the Battle of Trafalgar decorate the walls, including an original copy of the front page of *The Times* newspaper announcing the successful outcome of the battle. According to the cutting, just before engaging the enemy Nelson had said, 'Now they cannot escape us; I think we shall at least make sure of twenty of them. I shall probably lose a leg but that would be purchasing victory cheaply.' Taken below decks on being mortally wounded, Nelson turned to Captain Hardy and said '"I know I am dying, I could have wished to survive to breathe my last upon British ground, but the will

Houses on Argyle Place from Argyle Green (above).

of God be done." A few moments later he expired.'

A brasserie on the 1st floor of the hotel offers 'innovative Australian delights.' Elegant guest rooms on the top floor are decorated and furnished 'to capture the atmosphere of the colonial era.'

If you've survived the Lord Nelson and the Battle of Trafalgar, cross to the south east side of Kent Street where St Brigid's Church School has functioned as a school and 'occasional chapel' since 1835. Completed from 'stone which is close at hand', St Brigids, under the care of the Sisters of Mercy and the Marist Brothers, is the oldest Catholic building and Mass Centre in Australia still in use for its original purpose.

Observatory Hill

Head back around the corner into Argyle Street and fork right up Watson Road and Upper Fort Street to Observatory Hill. The low cliff surrounding Observatory Hill was formed when the surrounding area was quarried away for early Sydney buildings. The district around the hill was known at the time as 'The Quarries'. One one-eyed quarryman, George Herscot, was granted permission by the Town Surveyor to quarry stone by the hill 'on account of his being blown up… in the employ of Government.'

According to the Picturesque Atlas of Australia in 1886, when Observatory Hill was viewed from the harbour, above the busy wharves crowded with ships '…is the background of the

Locomotives for Australia's first railway line from Sydney to Parramatta were unloaded at Moore's Stores (above). The building is used by the Maritime Services Board and is not open to the public.

rising land, with the houses irregularly grouped, and the summit of the rock hill – the Acropolis of Sydney – crowned with the Observatory tower.'

Stroll on the grass on the north side of the hill past the 1912 band rotunda to the Boer War Memorial with its rusting Krupp artillery piece captured during the fighting, from where there's an excellent view of Argyle Place, Millers Point, the western harbour and along the length of Lower Fort Street to the Harbour Bridge. Fort Phillip wall nearby is worth more than a passing look because it is the oldest man-made structure in Sydney. In 1804, following an unsuccessful insurrection of Irish political prisoners at Castle Hill in west Sydney, Governor King ordered construction of a fort to use as a last line of defence in case of a further revolt by convicts or attack by the French. It was to be situated on Windmill Hill, which commanded an excellent defensive position on a 145 foot high conical hill just west of Sydney town, with clear fields of fire on all sides and a view over much of the harbour. Intended to mount 18 large cannon and named Fort Phillip Citadel 'in honour of Arthur Phillip Esq. Rear Admiral of the Blue', by August 1806 only two walls on the east side of the hexagonal sided fort were completed. The fort hadn't advanced much further during Bligh's term as Governor and eventually construction was abandoned altogether. Original plans for the fort were drawn up by Francis Barrallier, a French born engineer serving with the

New South Wales Corps who in the 1830s in London supervised the erection of Nelson's Column in Trafalgar Square. Rusted iron rings hanging from chains embedded in the fort wall were used to brace the tall flagstaff for the signal station which stood on the hill, one of a series of flag stations that operated between South Head and Parramatta for relaying messages. Governor Phillip originally erected a flagpole on the hill in July 1788 to signal the arrival of ships in the harbour. A sandstone lodge standing on the wall of the fort, designed by Colonial Architect Mortimer Lewis and completed in 1848, was used by the signal station staff.

When Governor Hunter arrived in Sydney in 1795 he carried on board his ship a pre-fabricated wooden windmill which was erected on a stone base on the site of the present day observatory. It was the first windmill in Sydney. Convicts carried their ration of grain up to the mill to be ground for flour, though the windmill was temporarily put out of action in June 1797 when a thief stole the canvas sails from the vanes. The hill is still marked as Windmill Hill on some of the current maps of Sydney.

Sydney Observatory

Follow Fort Phillip wall round to the entrance of the Observatory on the south side of the enclosure. Construction of the handsomely proportioned Sydney Observatory and Government Astronomer's Residence

The Lord Nelson "Sydney's oldest hotel" (above).

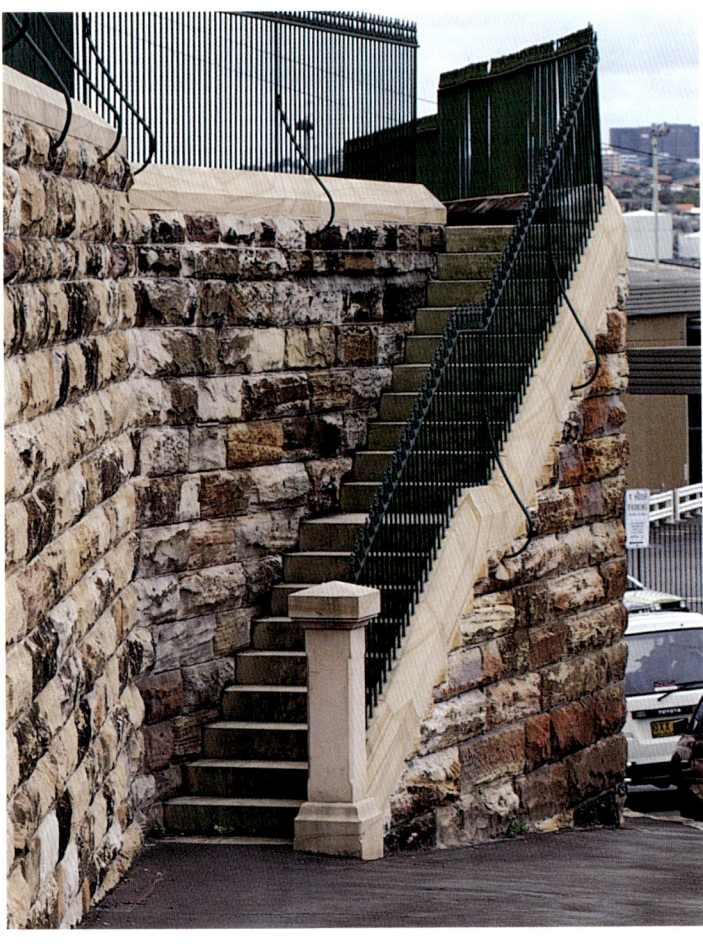

A restored stone terrace on Kent Street (above).

Stone steps on Dalgety Road (above right).

was completed in 1857 and 1859, and the telescope observatory towers with their rotating copper-sheathed domes on the north side of the building completed in 1877. It ceased being used as an observatory in 1982. The building is now operated by the Museum of Applied Arts and Sciences as an astronomical museum. The telescopes and some of the beautifully crafted original brass astronomical instruments are still in place. See George, the talking clock, 'At the third stroke it will be…' which for many years transmitted over telephone lines the voice of Australian broadcaster Gordon Gow who made the recordings in 1952. There are free tours of the telescope domes and you can study views of Sydney through the telescopes. The copper domes still rumble round on their original bearings of cannon balls. Will Dawes (the First Fleet astronomer and artillery officer) would have been proud! Be sure to pick up a paper on activities at the museum, with programs of night viewing of the moon, stars and planets through the telescopes.

When the Observatory tower was completed in 1858 a time ball on the weathervane dropped at 1 p.m. daily, 'sufficiently accurate for rating chronometers' as a signal for a gun to be fired from Fort Macquarie (at the site of the Opera House). When the fort was demolished for a tram depot at the turn of the century, the gun was then fired from Dawes Battery, and when the battery was abandoned the gun was fired from Fort Denison, a practice which ceased when anti-aircraft guns were mounted on the fort in February 1942. Firing of the 1 o'clock gun started again in 1986, and the dropping of the time ball (now on the sound of the gun) in 1987, though the dropping of the ball is subject to availability of staff and mechanical malfunctions.

Leave the Observatory and continue along Upper Fort Street. From this part of the hill there's a good view across the Harbour Bridge approach to Harry Seidler's grey Grosvenor Place building. At the point where Lower Fort Street swings to the right, on the left hand side is an open-air fenced enclosure containing the automatic meteorological recording equipment that measures Sydney's daily temperature and rainfall. For the record; Sydney's lowest ever recorded temperature was 2.1°C in 1932, highest 45.3°C in 1939, and highest rainfall during a 24 hour period 328 mm in 1986. Fortunately temperature extremes are rare in Sydney and it doesn't often reach over 36°C. Watkin Tench wrote of one hot day in February 1791 when 'the north-west wind... set in, and blew with great violence for three days... An immense flight of bats, driven before the wind, covered all the trees around the settlement, whence they every moment dropped dead, or (were) in a dying state, unable longer to endure the burning state of the atmosphere. Nor did the perroquettes, though tropical birds, bear it better; the ground was strewed with them in the same condition as the bats.'

Aerial view of Observatory Hill (above), with Argyle Green and the Garrison Church on the left, the Observatory at centre and the National Trust Centre on the right. Terraced houses line Kent Street at the bottom of the picture, and the Museum of Contemporary Art on Circular Quay can be picked out at the top of the picture.

Lower Fort Street and the Harbour Bridge from Observatory Hill.

Sydney Observatory (above) functioned as an astronomical observatory from 1858 to 1982 when it became a museum.

Corbels over the doors and windows of the Observatory (above left).

Fort Phillip wall (above right) is the oldest man-made structure in Sydney, dating to 1804.

A tablet on the Observatory tower (above) testifies that the building was erected in 1858 under the Governor Generalship of Sir William Denison.

The memorial to New South Wales volunteers killed in the Boer War (lower right).

The National Trust Centre

Walk along the path signposted to the Field Studies Centre, and cross the pedestrian bridge over the Cahill Expressway to the National Trust Centre. As you enter the Centre note the 'GR1815' inscribed in the keystone above the fanlight, testimony to the core of the building which was originally a two level military hospital with wide verandahs on both levels (similar to The Mint on Macquarie Street) built on the order of Governor Macquarie. The hospital closed in 1848 when Victoria Barracks in Paddington opened with its own hospital. The military hospital was designed by John Watts, an Irishman originally articled to a Dublin architect who had served in the Napoleonic Wars and the West Indies before being posted to Sydney as a Lieutenant with the 46th Regiment. Watts was appointed aide-de-camp to Macquarie, and when Watts returned to London in 1823 he married Jane Campbell, a relative of Macquarie's wife Elizabeth Campbell. Watts later returned to Australia and was postmaster of Adelaide from 1841 to 1861, though he never returned to New South Wales, passing away in South Australia in 1873.

The old hospital was remodelled in 1849 by Colonial Architect Mortimer Lewis by enclosing the verandahs with a new neo-classical facade – generally considered as Lewis' worst architectural effort. The building then became the first model school of the new

Board of National Education, and continued in use as the Fort Street School from 1849 to 1974.

Inside the National Trust Centre is the National Trust Shop, selling 'Australiana, Gifts and Books on Art and Architecture', and the National Trust Centre Cafe in one of the old classrooms. You may need to book for lunch on a weekday because it fills up rapidly with office workers from the City which is just five minutes walk away.

Walk through the cafe to the S.H. Ervin Gallery, located in a single storey Georgian style brick building built onto the rear of the school in 1857. The Gallery is named after Harry Ervin, who lived in a house at Mosman close to the squatter camp on Sirius Cove and befriended the artists Tom Roberts and Arthur Streeton who inhabited shacks at the camp. Ervin became a prosperous wool-buyer, and left a sum in his will when he passed away in 1977 for the National Trust to buy and exhibit Australian paintings. One of the well-known paintings owned by the gallery is *Circular Quay 1855* by Conrad Martens. The painting was done from Dawes Point, and Campbell's Stores are prominent in the picture without its top level which was added later.

Kent Street

Leave from the gallery by the outside door and take the road on the left, turning sharp left after 40 metres to descend the picturesque Agar Steps

The grassy knoll of Observatory Hill (above) is one of the most picturesque spots in Sydney. The bandstand on the right dates to 1912.

The Georgian style building (above) built as an extension to Fort Street School in 1857 was known as "the bulge" by generations of pupils. These days the building houses the S.H.Ervin Art Galllery.

leading to Kent Street. The steps are named after Thomas Agar, a local resident who settled in the area in the 1820s. Kent Street was known as Back Soldier's Row until renamed by Macquarie after the Duke of Kent, Queen Victoria's father. (The Duke died six days before his father, George III, and they were buried together on the same night in a vault at Windsor Castle.) The undulating terrain of the original cart track was later quarried level, leaving some of the houses perched high and dry above the street. One of these is Glover's Cottage built in 1820 at 124 Kent Street built by Thomas Glover on land granted to him by Governor Macquarie, and nick-named The Ark. Nearby at 120 Kent Street, also perched up on a rock, is Richmond Villa. The building was designed by Colonial Architect Mortimer Lewis for his own home on Hospital Road with a view of the Domain. The land on which it stood adjoined the New South Wales Parliament building, and the Government bought the villa in 1880 and used it for various purposes including the Sydney headquarters of the New South Wales Country Party from 1922 to 1957. When the site of the villa was needed for an extension to the New South Wales Parliament in 1975, the villa was dismantled stone by stone and re-erected on its present site where it re-opened in 1978 as headquarters of the Australian Society of Genealogists. The Genealogists are a useful first port of call for anyone wishing to trace their family tree.

A little further up Kent Street on the west side is a pub called the Dumbarton Castle which has a brasserie and a view from the lounge towards the docks and Balmain. The Dumbarton Castle along with the Harbour View and Palisade Hotel in Millers Point were built during a reconstruction program in The Rocks area by the Sydney Harbour Trust in the 1920s. For something with a bit more style try the Observatory Hotel on Kent Street opposite Agar Steps which has a comfortable bar and coffee lounge with its own library.

Bridge Stairs

Climb Agar Steps to return to Observatory Hill. Two large blocks of apartments nearby were once the I.B.M. Building (left) and Esso Building (right) converted to residential use in the 1990s following a glut in office space during the Great Recession of 1989 to 1993. Keep on the path to the left of the Observatory, enjoying the view of Millers Point and the western harbour, to return to Upper Fort Street. Walk through the subway on the corner marked Bridge Stairs which goes beneath the Bradfield Highway. You will come out in Cumberland Street at the stairs leading up to the pedestrian footpath on the Harbour Bridge. A 300 metre walk on the bridge footway with a magnificent view of The Rocks and Campbell's Cove takes you to the south east example of one of the 'Pillars of Hercules bestriding the tide' as *The Sydney Morning Herald* ecstatically describe the bridge pylons when the Harbour Bridge opened in 1932. A steel staircase through the hollow 89 metre high pylon leads to 'A fascinating display of how this modern Wonder of the World was built' with a description of the history of the bridge, photographs of early bridge designs and the mammoth task of construction. Construction of the grey granite facing for the approach piers and pylons was quite a feat in itself, involving the quarrying of 40,000 blocks from 18,000 cubic metres of stone from Moruya on the New South Wales south coast. Two hundred and fifty workers, mostly Scottish and Italian stonemasons brought specially out to Australia for the job, lived in a newly built village called 'Granite Town' near the Moruya quarry, that had 72 cottages, a store, hall, school and post office. Each stone was cut to size and finished at the quarry, then numbered for fitting on the construction site. Leftovers from the quarry were crushed and used in aggregate for the concrete of the approach piers and pylons.

Sydney Harbour Bridge

On 13th July 1788, the First Fleet transport *Alexander* left Sydney for England carrying Governor Phillip's dispatches to the home Government and the manuscript of a book. The manuscript was read by Erasmus Darwin, a doctor of medicine, botanist and poet, who wrote the epigraph for the official volume published in 1789 *The Voyage of Governor Phillip to Botany Bay*. The epigraph included the passage.

> '...*There the proud arch, Colussus-like bestride*
>
> *Yon glittering streams, and bound the chafing tide...*'

The poem for the epigraph was titled Visit of Hope to Sydney Cove. Erasmus Darwin (1731-1802) was the grandfather of Charles Darwin, (1809-1882) author of The Origin of the Species (1859), who later travelled to Sydney on board The Beagle in 1841.

The first proposal for a bridge across the harbour was put by convict architect Francis Greenway, who suggested to Macquarie in 1815 a bridge be 'thrown across from Dawes Battery to the North Shore.' A bridge could never have been a practical possibility at that time, and it wasn't until 1857 that the first known drawing for a bridge was produced, by Peter Henderson, a British immigrant engineer who had served his apprenticeship in George Stephenson's railway workshop in England. But it wasn't until the 1880s that serious consideration was given to the construction of a crossing. Since 1884 access to the north shore had been possible by road along the so-called 'five bridges route' across the Pyrmont, Glebe Island, Iron Cove, Gladesville and Fig Tree bridges, a distance of 12 miles, but by far the quickest way to cross the harbour was on one of the numerous vehicle and passenger ferries plying the waters. In 1890 the railway from Hornsby to Milsons Point opened, and that year ferries carried five million people, 43,800 horsemen, and 378,500 carriages and carts across the harbour. A Royal Commission charged with investigating alternatives for a harbour crossing recommended in 1890 'the connection shall be by a high-level bridge not obstructing the navigation of the harbour' rejecting a tunnel 'in face of the fact that so little is known as to what the waters of the harbour hide from view.' Over the following years numerous bridge proposals were canvassed, some almost going ahead, but all were rejected as being impractical or were shelved following a change in Government. One scheme proposed cutting a broad canal between Neutral Bay and Lavender Bay spanned by a level bridge across the high ground at North Sydney with the fill from the excavation used to build a road and rail causeway across the harbour between Dawes and Milsons Point.

Bradfield

In 1912 Parliament appointed Dr John Job Crew Bradfield to advise the Government on the design of a metropolitan electric rail system and a Harbour Bridge crossing between the city and North Sydney. Queensland born Bradfield obtained a Bachelor of Engineering at Sydney University with first-class honours, winning the University Gold Medal, and on the way was awarded the Levy Scholarship

The harbour bridge approach off the Cahill Expressway is chisselled out of the solid sandstone of Observatory Hill.

for Chemistry, the Smith Prize for Physics and the Sulman Prize for Architecture. In 1912 Bradfield was a design engineer with the New South Wales Public Works Department who cherished an 'ambition and ideal' for a bridge crossing the harbour, convinced that Sydney would become 'a New York in miniature' as soon as the 'lack of adequate transport facilities across the harbour had been alleviated.'

In 1914 Bradfield travelled Europe and North America studying underground rail systems and long span bridges, returning to Australia after the start of the First World War and completing his proposal for a Harbour Bridge in 1916. Though Parliament recommended a cantilever bridge for the crossing and following the war tenders were invited and received for this type of structure, Bradfield was convinced a large scale arch design held economic and technical advantages, apparently after seeing fabrication and erection methods used for the Hell Gate arch bridge in America, and asked the original Harbour Bridge tenderers to submit plans for an arch

Victorian Terraces line Agar Steps (above), which lead down from Observatory Hill to Kent Street.

design. Twenty different designs were received from six companies, and out of seven proposals by the Middlesborough, U.K. firm of Dorman Long & Co., Bradfield accepted scheme 'A3', a two hinged steel arch bridge with granite faced pylons, for a price of £4,217,721.11 shillings and 10 pence. At that time Dorman Long & Co owned the largest iron and steel works in the British Empire, employed 50,000 people in the U.K. and in its other branches around the globe, and had a direct involvement in many heavy construction projects.

Dorman Long & Co's design was to Dr Bradfield's specification, with the detailed design and erection scheme for the bridge carried out by Ralph Freeman of consulting engineers 'Sir Douglas Fox and Partners' (later Sir Ralph of Freeman Fox and Partners). The design of the pylons was by architects Sir John Burnet and Partners of London, and Lawrence Ennis of Dorman Long was appointed Director of Construction of the bridge and approaches.

Bridge Construction

First sod for the bridge was turned on the site of North Sydney Railway Station on 28th July 1923, eight months before formal acceptance of Dorman Long's tender on 24th March 1924. Massive workshops built at the site of the original Milsons Point Railway Station (at the present site of Luna Park) housed the heavy equipment for fabrication of bridge steel. In the 'heavy' and 'light' engineering shops, each of which was over 150 metres long, the steel was worked on massive drilling, machining and planing machines, and moved with great cranes including two of 120 ton capacity in the heavy workshop. Steel for the bridge was unloaded directly at the workshops by crane from steamers berthing alongside. Construction of the bridge with a single span 503 metres long carrying road, rail, tram and pedestrian traffic was only made possible at all, according to Lawrence Ennis, through the advent of special silicon steel with a strength 30% greater than mild steel. The ore for this steel, mined in the Cleveland Hills 'where Captain Cook… was born and raised as a boy' could only be forged at Dorman Long's works, so some 40,000 tonnes of silicon steel was rolled in England and 14,000 tonnes of mild carbon steel for the approaches and bridge deck were rolled at Australian steelworks at Newcastle and Port Kembla. There were to be no welded or bolted joints in the bridge, and 6,000,000 rivets, weighing 3,200 tonnes, were manufactured by McPherson's of Melbourne. Keeping all the fabrication work for the bridge in Australia ensured a maximum use of local labour with an average of 1,400 men employed on site through the construction period. The great depression had set in during construction and the number of workers employed was kept as high as possible by reducing the weekly working hours from 44 to 33.

To avoid erecting framework in the harbour channel to support the bridge arch while it was under construction, the arch was built in two halves, each held back by 128 steel cables anchored by 36 metre long horseshoe-shaped tunnels cut through the rock on the north and south shore. To construct the arch two giant creeper cranes weighing 580 tonnes with a lifting capacity of 120 tonnes built the arch in front of them as they went, starting at the deck level of the pylons and 'creeping' forward like a leviathan railway carriage up the slope of the crown of the arch. Erection of the arch started on 26th October 1928, and by 4th August 1930 the two halves were ready to be joined, seeming to defy gravity as they hung over the harbour with only a metre gap between them. Carefully co-ordinated progressive slackening of the restraining cables to 'close the gap' went on around the clock. On 13th August, before the gap was closed, Sydney was buffeted by 110 kilometre an hour gales and Lawrence Ennis at the top of one of the arches supervising the work watched in awe as the suspended arms, each weighing 15,000 tonnes gently swayed 7.5 cms from side to side in the wind. Fortunately, the bridge withstood this severe test at a critical phase of construction. The two halves touched for the first time at 4.15 p.m. on 19th August 1930, only to re-open again as the restraining cables and steel of the bridge contracted in the cool of the evening, and it was only at 10 p.m. that night that the gap was closed permanently. The following morning the Australian flag and Union Jack were flown from the jibs of the creeper cranes and ferries blew their sirens and passengers cheered as they rode across the harbour to work. Every worker involved in slackening the cables was given a gold sovereign and all workers were given a half-day off and two shillings to 'toast the bridge.'

Now the creeper cranes had the task of winching up the hanger and deck steel, from barges on the harbour, hanging the sections from the highest point of the arch back to the pylons to save moving the creeper cranes back, forward to the crown, then bfack again on completion.

Following the placing of the last stone on the top parapet on the north west pylon on 15th January 1932, and the asphalting of the road deck and laying of rail and tram lines, the bridge was ready for test loading in February. With extensometers and strain gauges in place, 96 steam locomotives weighing 7,560 tons were placed buffer to

Glover's Cottage on Kent Street (top) dates to 1820.

The National Trust Centre (above) was erected originally as a military hospital in 1815 and had a neo-classical facade added in 1848 when it was converted to a school.

53

buffer on the rail and tram tracks. Different load configurations were tried by removing trains from one side or one end, including one extreme test ordered by Bradfield of placing the entire 7,560 ton live load on the northern half of one side of the main span, notwithstanding the protests of Freeman and Ennis who pointed out this was nearly 20% beyond the design load for the bridge. Even so, deflections were less than calculated for in the design, and the bridge had proved more than capable of withstanding any load it was likely to bear.

The first to cross the bridge in a car was Bradfield with his daughter and two sons in the family Model A Ford in September 1931. Then on 19th January 1932 the first steam train crossed the bridge with Bradfield on the locomotive and Mrs Bradfield on the tender. Fifty thousand schoolchildren had the unofficial honour of opening the bridge on 16th March, 1932, three days before the official opening ceremony, when they queued in wellingtons and mackintoshes in pouring rain to wait for their turn to march across.

Francis de Groot

Before the official opening there were threats from a group called the New Guard that they planned to disrupt the opening ceremony. The New Guard were a right-wing organisation formed to counter the threat of communism, who had taken affront to the fact that the Labour Premier Jack Lang was to cut the ribbon to open the bridge instead of Royalty or the King's representative the Governor General. Captain Francis de Groot, an Irish migrant and member of the New Guard who had settled in Australia following the First World War, followed the Governor General's mounted escort onto the bridge on horse back wearing his old Hussar Regiment uniform and before Lang cut the ribbon spurred his horse forward and slashed through the ribbon with his sword declaring the bridge open 'On behalf of decent and loyal citizens of New South Wales.'

De Groot was bundled off his horse, arrested and charged, and at his trial found guilty of offensive behaviour in a public place and of injuring government property…'to wit one ribbon' and fined five pounds with four pounds costs. In his last known statement about the affair before he died in 1969 in a Dublin nursing home, de Groot said, 'I had opened the Harbour Bridge and that was all that mattered…'.

Following the official cutting of the opening ribbon a two kilometre long ceremonial procession with decorated floats and marchers followed an eight kilometre route through the city and over the bridge and back again. On the water, a 'Cavalcade of Shipping' led by ocean liners of different nations followed by hundreds of smaller craft were lined up stem to stern for a procession along the length of the harbour from the west side of the bridge. The biggest crowd ever gathered in Sydney took part in the spectacle as a million watched from the harbour shore or streets or took part in the festivities.

That night Sydney shook to the thunder of fireworks, blank rounds fired by the Royal Australian Navy ships and the sirens of liners. Warship searchlights illuminated the bridge and the harbour and city became a blaze of light and colour. Celebrations continued for the next twelve days.

At midnight on the 19th March, 1932, the first cars were allowed across the bridge. They paid a toll of 6 pence each. The original charges for other 'vehicles' were 3 pence for motorcycles or a horse and rider, 2 pence per head of cattle or 1 penny per head of sheep or pigs as loose stock.

Since it opened in 1932 the bridge has carried a far greater volume of traffic than was ever conceived when it was designed. Bradfield calculated that the bridge at maximum capacity could handle 6,000 vehicle crossings an hour on its six lanes. Now the figure in the morning peak hour is 12,774 vehicle crossing an hour (average on weekdays in 1993) on eight lanes. In 1959 two extra traffic lanes were opened on the east side of the bridge when the tram lines closed. This volume of traffic is made possible by a system of moveable median strips on the bridge approaches and flashing lights over the eight lanes on the bridge to allow a change of direction of traffic during peak hour to a six to two configuration. The overall length of the bridge of 1160 metres (three quarters of a mile) including approach spans, was named the Bradfield Highway in 1932 in honour of the 'Father of the Bridge' whose enthusiasm and drive pushed the project through from conception to completion. It is the shortest and busiest highway in Australia.

In his speech on the bridge opening day Bradfield mentioned 'My wife and children (who) freed me from home cares, and for the past twenty years the aim of my life has been to bring to fruition the function of today.'

Facts and Figures

The width of the deck of the Harbour Bridge at 49 metres earns it a place in the Guinness Book of Records as the widest large scale bridge in the world irrespective of method of construction.

When the Harbour Bridge was designed the length of its arch span of 503 metres would have been the longest in the world. But New York's

Campbell's Cove from the Pylon Lookout on the Harbour Bridge.

The Harbour Bridge under floodlights (above). When the floodlights were first turned on in 1961 the International Society of Illuminating Engineers declared the bridge was 'A joy for many... a filigree of light, a most delicate tracery spanning the blackness of the harbour.'

Bayonne Bridge, started after the Harbour Bridge and completed before it, is one metre longer. The Bayonne Bridge carries no rail traffic, and the weight of the steel in its arch at 16,250 tonnes is less than half that of the arch of the Sydney bridge at 39,000 tonnes. Currently, the longest steel arch bridge in the world is the New River Gorge bridge, West Virginia, U.S.A., completed in 1977 with a span of 518 metres.

Jack Lang also earns his place in the Guinness Book of Records as the longest lived Premier of an Australian state. Lang died in Sydney on 27th September 1975 aged 98. Not long after the opening of the bridge, on May 13th 1932, Jack Lang was sacked by the Governor Sir Philip Game. New South Wales had defaulted on payments to British bondholders, including loans for the Harbour Bridge, and the Australian Government assumed liability. The Australian Government passed a law to recover the money from New South Wales, but Lang, who was Colonial Treasurer as well as Premier, refused to pay, and he was dismissed from office. George V wrote to Game the following month, 'We are enchanted with your triumph over Lang and that in spite of New Guards, Old Guards and Red Guards, you have come into your own. From being the Villain of the Piece you have been exalted to Hero of the Day.'

The bridge toll was put in place to cover the construction cost of £10,057,170.00, which included land

The liner 'Asuka' approaching Sydney Cove as a harbour ferry passes beneath the Harbour Bridge.

acquisition and building the bridge approaches. For many years the toll remained a bargain, at the start of 1987 the toll was 20¢ a car (effectively 10¢ a crossing, the toll is paid to travel across from north to south, there is no charge to travel from south to north). On the 1st June 1987 the toll went up five times to a $1.00, amid fierce public protest, to pay for the new Sydney Harbour Tunnel. Not long after, the toll went up to $2.00, the same charge levied for a one-way traverse through the Harbour Tunnel which opened in 1992. The cost of the bridge itself was paid off by the Government in October 1988.

Return by the bridge footway and Bridge Stairs to Cumberland Street. Not far from the site of the stairs once stood Cumberland Place, a stately house designed by Francis Greenway for Robert Campbell demolished in the 1900s. Still standing on the opposite side of the road are two local watering holes, the Australian Hotel serving 'only Scharers Bavarian Style Draught Beer' and the Glenmore Hotel, both popular with office workers at lunchtime. The Glenmore has an open-air terrace with trestle tables on the flat roof with a good view of Circular Quay and the Opera House.

At 58-64 Gloucester Street near the Australian Hotel, is a terrace of houses built in 1844 by Irish immigrants Edward and Mary Riley in a similar style to the Irish terraced town housing they would have known at home. The terrace, called Susannah Place, is

The Rocks Square on Playfair Street (above).

named after their niece who accompanied them to New South Wales.

The Rocks Square

Take the steps on the right of the Glenmore Hotel to Gloucester Walk. Immediately on the right – but don't go down them – are Argyle Stairs, close to the location of the original Argyle Stairs cut into the sandstone of The Rocks by convicts in 1815 so pedestrians could climb over the ridge to Millers Point. Continue on Gloucester Walk past the rear of Immigration House, and descend on the right the steep steps through Foundation Park, built on the remains of Erin Terrace, eight small houses which stood on the site from 1875 to 1938. Walk through one of the passages through Argyle Terrace (1875-77) to The Rocks Square on Playfair Street. Argyle Terrace was built by Thomas Playfair, one time Lord Mayor of Sydney, for workers in his meat company. There is said to be a ghost in the terrace, but according to a shop tenant the ghost is quiet and friendly as she was a very old woman whose son had to carry her from her bedroom down the tiny steep narrow steps to the parlour below to be with the family. There are plenty of restaurants and Australiana shops on the square.

On the north side of the square (towards the bridge) stands the Westpac Museum opened on 8th of April 1987 to commemorate the 170th anniversary of the opening of Australia's first bank, the Bank of New

South Wales in 1817. The first branch of the Bank of New South Wales was opened on the ground floor of Mary Reiby's house on Macquarie Place. Mary Reiby's face now appears on the back of the Australian $20.00 note. The Bank of New South Wales was renamed 'Westpac' in 1982.

The Westpac Museum contains displays of coins and banknotes, including privately minted 'token' coinage unofficially and illegally produced but condoned because of the almost total lack of coinage in the infant colony. Significant events in the history of banking in Australia are shown against a background of illustrations of significant world events in the same years.

Atherden Street outside the museum, the shortest street in Sydney, was once called Union Street after the nearby Union Bond Stores then renamed Atherden after an early resident. The six terraces that George Atherden built in the 1850s were demolished when Playfair Street was widened in the 1920s. Four of the remaining terraces on the street were built by Thomas Playfair in the 1880s. Note the nearby sandstone *First Impressions* sculpture crafted by Bud Dumas in 1979 with incised figures on three sides of a convict, family and soldier.

Walk to the end of Atherden Street and turn left on George Street. The Merchants House built in 1848 at number 43, a Georgian townhouse built of sandstone by architect John Bibb is the only building of its kind still

Argyle Stairs (top left) lead from Argyle Street to Gloucester Walk and Bridge Stairs on Cumberland Street.

Atherden Street off Playfair Street (top right) is the shortest street in Sydney.

The Union Bond Stores (1841) on George Street (above left), containing a branch of the Wespac Bank, was designed by Ashley Alexander, designer of Dartmoor Prison in England.

'Sgt Majors Row' on George Street (above).

standing in The Rocks. The house was built for Martyn & Combes, 'painters, glaziers and plumbers' to operate their business from. Next door at 29-41 George Street, the Sergeant Major's Row terraces built 1881-1883, carry one of the early names for George Street.

Further up George Street not far from the Harbour Bridge approach is the 1914 to 1915 Mercantile Hotel, named after the Mercantile Rowing Club once located on Campbell's Cove. The pub has an Irish atmosphere and flies the flag, sings the songs and sells Guinness to this day. Note the original green Art Nouveau tiles of the exterior. Shops and restaurants occupy the lower levels of the 1912 Metcalf Stores on the opposite side of the road.

Argyle Stores

Backtrack along George Street and Playfair Street to Argyle Stores on the corner of Argyle Street, a wonderful collection of old stores some of which date back to the first decades of settlement. They feature huge doorways, solid sandstone and brick construction, great timber ceiling beams and the remnants of a water hydraulic hoist. Granite cobblestones in the courtyard off Argyle Street were brought out as ship's ballast in the 1840s. The store on the corner of Argyle Street was originally built by Captain John Piper and had its handsome dressed sandstone facade added when it was Sydney's second Customs House from 1830 to 1845. At the well-known Argyle Tavern near Argyle Cut workers swear that someone unseen moves the plates and cutlery from time to time. It could be the ghost of Mary Reiby, an ex-convict business woman who once owned that part of the stores. Reiby was transported at the age of thirteen for going on a joyride on a carthorse, and after marrying in Sydney took over her husband's business interests when he died in 1811 leaving Mary with seven children to bring up.

Cross Argyle Street to Harrington Street. The 1886 building on the south corner was once the British Seamen's Hotel – apparently *not* a brothel. Next door at 28 Harrington Street, Reynold's Cottage dates to the 1820s. The cottage was bought in 1830 by an Irish ex-convict William Reynolds who ran a blacksmith's forge in the back yard.

Suez Canal

On the left off Harrington Street is the stone paved Suez Canal, the narrowest laneway in Sydney, less than a metre wide at its southern end on George Street. The lane was referred to last century as 'Sewer Lane'. At the time drainage and sewerage in The Rocks relied on natural rainfall to carry it away. The more modern name appeared some time after the opening of the real Suez Canal, no doubt because of the torrents of water that raced down the lane after storms. The Suez Canal was one of the haunts of The Rocks Push, and only fools or gang members would venture there after dark. In the 1970s the body of a murdered underworld person was found in the boarded up terraced houses on the north side of Harrington Street. It had been there for some time, which led to its discovery!

Walk down Suez Canal. On the left are the tables and bistro of The Phillip's Foote pub, winner of the 'Best Garden Restaurant' award, located in a one time shop, customs agent and stables. If it's lunchtime you can barbecue your own T-bone steak, marinated pork rump or chicken breast or serve yourself salad at the brasserie.

On the far side of the restaurant courtyard Greenway Lane is named after convict architect Francis Greenway, who in 1815 was given permission to live in a house on the site built for the Assistant Surgeon of the nearby hospital. In England Greenway designed the Clifton Civic Centre during the short time he held an architectural practice from 1804 until his bankruptcy in 1809. Greenway didn't receive an official title to the Surgeon's House and was evicted by the Sheriff in 1834 and the Crown took possession. The present stone paved Greenway Lane dating to the 1840s led from Argyle Street to the stables of the buildings fronting George Street. The stone paving with ruts worn by carriage wheels was discovered beneath a coating of tar during restoration work in 1976.

The first hospital

Return to Suez Canal and cross it to Nurses Walk, a pleasant shady lane with several shops and cafes named after the nurses of the first hospitals which stood in the area from 1788 to 1816.

When the First Fleet left England Watkin Tench of the marines believed '…few Marines going out of England upon Service were ever so amply provided for as these Convicts are…'. On the transport *Scarborough* not a single person was lost on the passage to Botany Bay, and those that died on other ships were either infirm on departure or carried disease on board picked up while in prison in England. As the weather became hot and wet when the First Fleet entered the tropics, to maintain the health of the men and guard against 'impure air', 'Frequent explosions of gunpowder, lighting fires between decks, and a liberal use of that admirable antiseptic, oil of tar, were the preventives made use of…' (First Fleeter Watkin Tench).

Art deco tiles decorate the outside wall of the Mercantile Hotel (left).

Paving stones in the courtyard of the Argyle Stores (below) were brought out as ballast in sailing ships.

The Suez Canal (above) was once known as 'Sewer Lane'. It is the narrowest lane in Sydney.

The Harbour Rocks Hotel (above right) occupies an old stores building. Reynold's Cottage on the far left dating to the 1820's is named after ex-convict William Reynolds who operated a blacksmith's forge in the backyard.

On arrival at Sydney Cove a hospital was built on the west side of the Cove approximately at the site of the old Rocks Police Station, with its garden along the route of Nurses Walk. The hospital was built by 12 convict carpenters and 16 crew from First Fleet transports on the cove, but by November was still 'not half finished, nor fit to receive an object.' Governor Phillip wrote that 'soon after landing, a dysentery prevailed which in several instances proved fatal, and the scurvy began to rage with a virulence which kept the hospital tents generally supplied with patients.' A red gum from the locally growing giant angophora trees was found to be 'perfectly soluble in water… (and) a very powerful remedy' for the dysentery.

In June 1790 when the Second Fleet arrived, on board the *Justinian* was a military 'Moveable Hospital for His Majesty's distant possessions.' The pre-fabricated building, 50 metres long by 6 metres wide, was erected in just over a week at the hospital site and immediately crammed with sick from the Second Fleet who overflowed into 100 tents in the hospital grounds. The masters of the Second Fleet ships had withheld supplies from the convicts on board, which on arrival they sold from stalls set up near the cove. Of 1,038 convicts who had embarked with the Second Fleet, 273 had died on the passage out and of 486 landed sick in Sydney 124 died in the hospital.

Reverend Johnson wrote in a letter of boarding the Second Fleet vessel

P & O's 'Sea Princess' on Sydney Cove at dawn.

Surprise when it arrived in Sydney. 'Went down amongst the convicts, where I beheld a sight truly shocking to the feelings of humanity, a great number of them laying, some half and others nearly quite naked, without either bed or bedding, unable to turn or help themselves… the smell was so offensive that I could scarcely bear it… Some of these unhappy people died after the ships came into the harbour, before they could be taken on shore – part of these had been thrown into the harbour, and their dead bodies cast upon the shore, and were seen laying naked upon the rocks… The landing of these people was truly affecting and shocking; great numbers were not able to walk; nor to move hand or foot; such were slung over the ship side in the same manner as they would sling a cask, a box or anything of that nature. Upon their being brought up to the open air some feinted, some died upon deck, and others in the boat before they reached the shore.'

To return to the more happy present, continue to the end of Nurses Walk, turn left on Globe Street and cross George Street to First Fleet Park at Circular Quay, the starting point for this tour of The Rocks.

Index

References in brackets
refer to the map on Page 5

A.N.A. Hotel, 8, 9, (E7)
Aboriginal & Tribal Art Centre, 12
Adams, John, 28
Agar Steps, 50, 52, (C7)
Agar, Thomas, 50
Albert Chapman Gallery, 29
Alexander, 51
Alexander, Ashley, 59
Alfred Street, 6, (F7)
Alfred, Prince, 16
Alt, Baron (Surveyor), 30
Argyle Cut, 3, 37, 60, (D5)
Argyle Green, 37, 41, 45
Argyle Place, 34, 36, 38, 40, 41, 42, (B5)
Argyle Stairs, 58, 59, (E5)
Argyle Stores, 60, 61
Argyle Street, 14, 16, 37, 40, 41, 60, (A5)
Argyle Tavern, 60
Argyle Terrace, 58
Ark, 50
Ashfield, Laird of, 24
Asuka, 57
Atherden Street, 59, (F4)
Atherden, George, 59
Australasian Steam Navigation Company Stores, 22, 23, 24, (F3)
Australasian Steam Navigation Hotel, 14, 16
Australian Craftworks, 12
Australian Hotel, 57
Australian Society of Genealogists, 50

Back Soldier's Row, 50
Ball, R. T., 33
Bank of New South Wales, 59
Banks, Sir Joseph, 24, 27
Barnet, James, 12
Barney & Bligh Reserve, 17, 20, (F5)
Barney, George (Lieutenant Colonel), 20, 22
Barrallier, Frances, 42
Barret, Thomas, 7
Barton, Sir Edmund, 37
Bibb, John, 16, 59, 60
Bigge, Commissioner, 3
Blacket, Edmund, 36, 38
Bligh House, 34, (D3)
Bligh, Governor, 17, 20, 24, 26, 27, 28, 29, 42
Boer War Memorial, 42
Botany Bay, 2
Bounty, 19, 24, 25, 26, 28, 30
Bradfield Highway, 50, 54, (E1)
Bradfield, Dr. John Job Crew, 51, 54
Bridge Stairs, 50, 57, 59, (D5)
British Seamen's Hotel, 60
Brooklyn, 10
Burke, Governor, 37
Burnet, Sir John & Partners, 52

Cadman's Cottage, 16, 17, 19, 22, 23, (F5)
Cadman, John, 18
Cahill Expressway, 7, 10, 48, 51, (E7)
Campbell's Bank, 24
Campbell's Cove, 19, 24, 25, 28, 29, 30, 34, 50, 55 (F2)
Campbell's Stores, 22, 23, 24, 26, 29, 49
Campbell, Elizabeth, 48
Campbell, Jane, 48
Campbell, John, 24
Campbell, Robert Jnr., 34
Campbell, Robert, 24, 34, 57
Canberra, The, 23
Chapman, James, 14
Charlotte Place, 9
Christian, Fletcher, 27, 28

Chusan, s.s., 39
Circular Quay, 4, 6, 7, 14, 23, 24, 45, 57, 63, (G5)
City Morgue and Coroner's Court, 16
City of Sydney, 10
Clarence, Duke of, 10
Clark, Ralph, 3
Clarke, Jonathon, 35
Clutterbuck, Charles, 36
Collins, David, 3, 7
Colonial House Museum, 34
Combined Services Museum, 37
Commissariat Stores, 13, 15
Cook, Captain, 2, 24, 52
Coxswain's Barracks, 16, 19
Crystal Harmony, 1
Cumberland Place, 57
Cumberland Street, 9, 34, 50, 57 (E3)
Customs Officers Stairs, 24, (F3)
Cutty Sark, 14

D.F.S. Duty Free, 10
Dadswell, Lyndon, 14, 24
Dalgety Road, 44
Darling Harbour, 4, 31
Darlinghurst Gaol, 9
Darwin, Charles, 51
Darwin, Erasmus, 51
Davis, William, 10
Dawes Point Battery, 30, 33, 36, 44
Dawes Point Park, 21, 28, 30, 31, 33, 34, (F1)
Dawes Point, 30, 31, 37, 49, (D2)
Dawes, Lieutenant William, 30, 33, 35, 44
de Chair, Governor Sir Dudley, 33
de Groot, Francis, 54
Denison, Sir William, 48
Dog Lane, 3
Dorman Long & Co., 52
Dumas, Bud, 59
Dumbarton Castle, 50

Earth Exchange, 23, 27, 29, (E3)
Elizabeth Bay House, 34
Elizabeth Henrietta, 16
Ennis, Lawrence, 52, 53, 54
Erin Terrace, 58
Ervin, Harry, 49
Essex Street, 7, 8, 9, (D8)
Esso Building, 50

Ferry Lane, 4, 36
Field Studies Centre, 48
First Fleet Park, 7, 63, (F7)
First Fleet, 2, 3, 23, 28, 30, 51, 60, 62
First Impressions, 59
Five Bridges Route, 51
Flying Fish, 18
Fort Denison, 44
Fort Macquarie, 44
Fort Phillip Wall, 42, 43, 45, 48
Fort Street School, 49, 50
Fortune of War Hotel, 12
Fortune of War Inn, 12, 13
Foundation Park, 58
Foveaux, Lieutenant Colonel, 14
Fox, Sir Douglas & Partners, 52
Franklin, F. A., 4
Freeman, Ralph, 7, 52, 54
Friendship, 3
Frog Hollow, 3

Garrison Church (Church of Holy Trinity), 35, 36, 37, 38, 39, 45, (D5)
Geological & Mining Museum, 29
George Street, 6, 10, 11, 12, 13, 14, 16, 24, 34, 59, 60, 63 (F4)
Gladstone Hotel, 3

Glenmore Hotel, 57, 58, (E5)
Globe Hotel, 10
Globe Street, 10, 12, 63, (F7)
Gloucester Street, 9, 57, 59, (D7)
Gloucester Walk, l58, 59
Glover's Cottage, 50, 53
Glover, Thomas, 50
Government Astronomer's Residence, 43
Government Coxswain, 18
Government Dockyard, 16
Government Ordinance Stores, 24
Gow, Gordon, 44
Great Eastern, The, 14
Greenway Lane, 60, (F5)
Greenway, Francis, 16, 51, 57, 60
Grinn, Henry, 36
Grosvenor Hotel, 9
Grosvenor Place, 8, 9, 10, 45, (E9)
Grosvenor Street, 10, (D9)
Grubb, W. A., 10

Harbour Rocks Hotel, 62, (F5)
Harbour View Hotel, 34, 50
Harbour Watch, 30
Harrington Stores, 14
Harrington Street, 3, 8, 10, 60 (E6)
Harris, Alexander, 3
Harts Pubs, 9
Hayes, Michael, 3
Hayward, Lieutenant, 27
Haywood, Elizabeth, 2
Henderson, Peter, 51
Herald Square, 6, 7, (F7)
Hercules, The, 22
Hero of Waterloo, 3, 35, 36, (C4)
Herscot, George, 41
Hickson Road, 23, 24, 29, 30, 31, 33, 34, (F1)
Hickson, Commissioner, 33
High Street, 11
Hit or Miss, 3
Horizons Bar, 9
Horse Ferry Dock, 30
Hudson, John, 2
Hughes, Billy, 4
Hunter, Governor, 3, 43
Hunter, The, 24
Hyde Park Barracks, 3, 37

I.B.M. Building, 50, (C9)
Immigration House, 58
Island Princess, The, 6

James, Edith Mary, 12
Jamieson Street, 10, (D10)
Jevons, Stanley, 4
Johnson's Building, 10
Johnson, Reverend Richard, 2, 62
Johnstone, Major, George, 20, 24
Jubilee Nugget, 29
Justinian, The, 62

Ken Done Gallery, 24
Kent Street, 38, 40, 41, 44, 45, 49, 50, 52, 53, (B4)
King, Governor, 11, 42
King, Lieutenant, 2
Lady Penrhyn, 2

Lang Park, 8, 10, (D10)
Lang, John Dunmore, 10
Lang, Premier Jack, 54, 56
Lawson, Henry, 3
Leighton, John, 35
Lewis, Mortimer, 43, 48, 50
Lilyvale Cottage, 8, 9
Long, William, 39
Lord Nelson Hotel, 39, 39, 40, 41, 43, (B5)

64